Nicolae Sfetcu

ELECTRONIC WARFARE
and
ARTIFICAL INTELLIGENCE

MultiMedia

Bucharest, 2024

DOI: 10.58679/MM14430

MultiMedia
Bucharest, 2024
Email: office@multimedia.com.ro

Sfetcu, Nicolae (2024), Electronic Warfare and Artificial Intelligence,
MultiMedia Publishing, ISBN 978-606-033-844-4, DOI: 10.58679/MM14430,
https://www.telework.ro/ro/e-books/electronic-warfare-and-artificial-
intelligence/

CONTENTS

ABSTRACT

Electronic warfare is a critical component of modern military operations and has undergone significant advances in recent years. This book provides an overview of electronic warfare, its historical development, key components, and its role in contemporary conflict scenarios. It also discusses emerging trends and challenges in electronic warfare and its contemporary relevance in an era of advanced technology and cyber threats, emphasizing the need for continued research and development in this area.

The book explores the burgeoning intersection of artificial intelligence and electronic warfare, highlighting the evolving landscape of modern conflicts and the implications of integrating advanced technologies. The multifaceted roles of artificial intelligence in electronic warfare are highlighted, examining its potential advantages, ethical considerations, and challenges associated with its integration.

Keywords: electronic warfare, artificial intelligence, machine learning, cognitive warfare, asymmetric warfare, electromagnetic spectrum

ABBREVIATIONS

AI = Artificial Intelligence
ANN = Artificial Neural Network
C&C = Command and Control
CDP = Capability Development Plan
CEW = Cybernetic Electronic Warfare
CNN = Convolutional Neural Network
CNO = Computer Network Operations
COMINT = Communication Intelligence
CW = Cyber Warfare
DE = Directed Energy
DL = Deep Learning
DNN = Deep Neural Network
DoD = US Department of Defense
EA = Electronic Attack
ECCM = Electronic Counter-countermeasures
ECM = Electronic Countermeasure
EDA = European Defence Agency
ELINT = Electronic Intelligence
EM = Electromagnetic
EME = Electromagnetic Environment
EMOE = Electromagnetic Operational Environment
EMS = Electromagnetic Spectrum
EMSO = Electromagnetic Spectrum Operations
EOB = Electronic Order of Battle
EP = Electronic Protection
EPM Electronic Protective Measures
ES = Electronic Warfare Support
ESM = Electronic Support Measures

EW = Electronic Warfare
IoT = Internet of Thinngs
ISR = Intelligence, Surveillance and Reconnaissance
JADC2 = US Joint All Domain Command and Control
JEMSO = Joint Electromagnetic Spectrum Operations
LAWS = Lethal Autonomous Weapon Systems
MILDEC = Military Deception
ML - Machine Learning
MLP = Multi-Layer Perceptron
NDS = US National Defense Strategy
OPSEC = Operations Security
PSYOP = Psychological Operations
RF = Radio Frequency
SIGINT = Signal Intelligence
UAV = Unmanned Aerial Vehicle (drone)

INTRODUCTION

Electronic warfare (EW) is a critical component of modern military operations and has undergone significant advances in recent years. It is a multifaceted field of warfare that involves manipulating the electromagnetic (EM) spectrum to gain a tactical advantage.

The recent explosive development of emerging technologies has radically changed war strategies. As the modern battlespace has become more sophisticated, military operations are executed in an increasingly complex electromagnetic environment. Military operations now depend heavily on controlling the electromagnetic spectrum that can disrupt the flow of data by targeting, exploiting, degrading, deceiving, damaging, or destroying adversary electronic systems. The part of the electromagnetic spectrum of the information environment is called electromagnetic environment (EME).

In this context, gaining and maintaining an advantage in modern warfare requires a range of EW solutions, new solutions that can target and exploit system vulnerabilities, and that can significantly alter military deception operations (MILDEC), improving joint operations and C&C warfare.

Artificial intelligence has developed explosively in recent years, with applications such as object recognition, natural language processing, and automatic speech recognition. Machine learning (ML) techniques have generated interest in EW for emitter identification, autonomous resource allocation, and automation.

The emergence of artificial intelligence has revolutionized various fields, and electronic warfare is no exception.

1 ELECTRONIC WARFARE

Electronic warfare (EW) assists air, ground, naval, and space forces at multiple levels of conflict by limiting the use of the radio frequency (RF) spectrum (Lazarov 2019). A nation's defense system relies on EMS for its command and control (C&C) infrastructure, communications links, weapon systems, and support technologies.

EW enables kinetic warfare, which is simply ineffective in modern warfare without EW (Duke 2023).

DEFINITIONS

Electronic warfare (EW) includes "Military action involving the use of electromagnetic and directed energy to control the electromagnetic spectrum or to attack the enemy." (Army 2016).

Electronic warfare includes three major subdivisions: electronic attack (EA), electronic protection (EP), and electronic warfare support (ES) (Army 2000, sec. I–1).

Electronic warfare refers to the use of electronic means in EMS to disrupt, deny, degrade, or deceive an adversary's information or communications systems without causing physical damage (Army 1996).

Information: Facts, data, or instructions in any medium or form. Information also refers to the meaning a human assigns to data through the known conventions used in representing it (Army 2016).

Information Operation (IO): IO is described as the integrated engagement of electronic warfare (EW), computer network operations (CNO), psychological operations (PSYOP), military deception (MILDEC), and operations security (OPSEC), along with specified support and related capabilities, to influence, disrupt, corrupt, or usurp adversarial and automated human decision-making while protecting us (Army 2020a).

Information Warfare (IW): Information operations conducted during a crisis or conflict to achieve or advance specific objectives on an adversary.

Information superiority: A state of equilibrium in one's favor in the information domain (Army 2020b, 8) or the operational advantage derived from the ability to collect, process, and disseminate an uninterrupted flow of information while exploiting or denying an adversary's ability to do the same (Army 2016, 257).

Information environment: The aggregate of people, organizations and systems that collect, process, disseminate or act on information (Army 2016, 257).

Electromagnetic environment: The resultant product of the power and time distribution, over various frequency ranges, of the levels of radiated or directed electromagnetic emissions likely to be encountered by a military force, system or platform when performing its assigned mission in its intended operational environment. It is the sum of electromagnetic interference; electromagnetic pulse; electromagnetic radiation hazards to personnel, artillery and volatile materials; and the effects of natural phenomena of lightning and static precipitation (Army 2016, 175).

Operational electromagnetic energy: A combination of the strength, frequency, and duration of electromagnetic emissions that may be encountered by a military force while performing its assigned mission (Army 2000, sec. I–1).

Directed energy: A general term that defines technologies related to the production of a beam of concentrated electromagnetic energy, atomic particles, or subatomic particles. It is used to damage or destroy an adversary's equipment, personnel, and installations (Army 2000, sec. I–4).

Electronic Intelligence (ELINT): The intelligence obtained from non-communicative external EM radiation. Electronic intelligence can be technical, geospatial or both (Kucukozyigit 2006).

Electronic security: The activity aimed at prohibiting unauthorized persons from accessing valuable information, resulting in the protection of friendly systems against activities such as interception or non-communications radiation (Kucukozyigit 2006).

Electronic reprogramming: Represents changes to EW and target-sensitive systems to accommodate changes in equipment, tactics, and the EM environment. These changes can be due to friendly or hostile activities. The desired outcome of electronic reprogramming is to support and increase the effectiveness of sensitive EW and targeting systems and devices used in defensive or offensive weapons and intelligence collection systems (Kucukozyigit 2006).

Emission Control (EMCON): The selective and controlled use of EM, acoustic and other emitters to achieve optimal C&C capabilities

(Kucukozyigit 2006).

Spectrum management: is the planning, coordination and management of the EM spectrum. The objective is to create an EM environment in which friendly electronic systems can perform their functions without interference or confusion (Army 2000, sec. I-6–7).

HISTORICAL DEVELOPMENT

Electronic warfare has its roots in early radio and radar technologies. They can be traced back to the US Civil War since 1861. With the outbreak of the Civil War in 1861, telegraph wires became one of the most important targets. Military telegraph traffic was diverted to the wrong destinations, false orders were passed to Union commanders, and wires were cut to intercept information to Union forces (Price 1984, 1–2). These can be considered early applications of command, control, communications and intelligence (C3I), early examples of intelligence, jamming and deception (J. P. R. Browne and Thurbon 1998, 3).

The earliest documented use of EW was during the Boer War (1899–1902), when the British Army used a searchlight for Morse code signals from the clouds. The Boers noticed this and used one of their own searchlights in an attempt to jam the British signals (Judd and Surridge 2013).

The first known case of intentional jamming was, surprisingly, not for military purposes, but for civilian purposes, during the 1901 America's Cup yacht races in the United States. That year, Marconi obtained a contract from the Associated Press. Another company, the Wireless Telegraph Company of America, also won a contract. A third company, the American Wireless Telephone and Telegraph Co., was unable to secure a sponsor, so it decided to jam the others using a more powerful transmitter (Price 1984, 3).

The first intentional use of radio jamming by the military occurred in 1902 during British naval exercises in the Mediterranean, then in 1903 during US naval maneuvers (Price 1984, 4).

During the Russo-Japanese War of 1904–1905, the Japanese located the Russian fleet in the Tsushima Strait and transmitted the information "wirelessly" to the Japanese fleet headquarters. On July 13, 1904, Russian wireless telegraph stations successfully disrupted communication between a group of Japanese battleships. This was also the first example of electronic countermeasures. Later, the captain of the Russian warship Ural requested permission to disrupt Japanese communications with a stronger radio signal, but Russian Admiral Zinovy Rozhestvensky refused, thus allowing the Japanese to win a decisive battle at Tsushima (Rambo 2009).

During World War I and World War II, EW primarily involved radio jamming and radar deception. In 1939, just before the outbreak of World War II, the first ELINT mission was carried out by the German airship Graf Zeppelin along the east coast of Great Britain (Kucukozyigit 2006).

In World War II, the Allies turned to EW in the "Battle of the Beams", using navigational radars to direct bombers, with adversaries attempting to defeat those navigational radars (Rambo 2009). Chaff was used by the Royal Air Force (code name Window) during World War II to defeat radar tracking systems (McArthur 1990). In the first example of ECCM, the Germans increased the power of their radio transmitter in an attempt to "get through" or overcome British jamming, and this is still one of the main methods of ECCM today.

The Cold War era saw substantial advances in electronic warfare as the superpowers engaged in a technological arms race to overcome each other's surveillance and communications systems. Cold War developments included anti-radiation missiles designed to target enemy radar transmitters (Polmar 1979).

In the first example of ECCM, the Germans increased the power of their radio transmitter in an attempt to "get through" or overcome British jamming, and this is still one of the main methods of ECCM today.

The Cold War era saw substantial advances in electronic warfare as superpowers engaged in a technological arms race to outsmart each other's surveillance and communications systems. Cold War developments included anti-radiation missiles designed to target enemy radar transmitters (Polmar 1979).

During the Korean War (1950–1953) under General Mac Arthur, the US deployed 100 B-29 Superfortress heavy bombers to the theater of war. The North Koreans installed early warning radars and radar-controlled anti-aircraft artillery (AAA), so that aircraft losses became unacceptable (J. P. R. Browne and Thurbon 1998, 26).

Electronic warfare also played a major role during the Vietnam War, where aircraft often relied on EW to survive the battle, although the Vietnamese ECCM operated successfully (Dickson 1987).

In the First Gulf War (Operation DESERT STORM) in 1991, stealth fighters ventured into enemy airspace dropping decoys to trigger enemy radar into action; some carrying anti-radiation missiles that activated instantly as the radars appeared (Campen 1992, XIV).

In 2007, an Israeli strike during Operation Outside the Box (or Operation Orchard) used EW to disrupt Syria's air defenses (Fulghum and Wall 2007) (Katz 2010).

In the early days of the Russian invasion of Ukraine in 2022, Russian EW disrupted enemy radars and communications, disrupting ground-based air defense systems as well as their own communications (Bronk, Reynolds, and Watling 2022). Russian ability to disrupt GPS signals is credited with reducing the success of Ukrainian use of HIMARS and JDAM bombs (Mizokami 2023). According to a report by the Royal United Services Institute on May 19, 2023, Ukraine had lost approximately 10,000 drones per month due to Russian electronic warfare (Jankowicz 2023).

In modern warfare, electronic warfare has become a critical component. With the integration of sophisticated sensors, communication systems and information networks, the electromagnetic spectrum is crowded and contested. EW plays a vital role in gaining the edge in terms of situational awareness and tactical advantage.

EW in asymmetric warfare: EW is not exclusive to conventional warfare. It has gained importance in asymmetric conflicts, counterinsurgency operations, and counterterrorism efforts. Insurgent groups and non-state actors have also adopted rudimentary electronic warfare techniques.

Cyber-electronic convergence: The convergence of cyber warfare and electronic warfare has seen significant development. Adversaries are increasingly using cyber-attacks to disrupt electronic systems, blurring the lines between the two domains.

Space and electromagnetic spectrum dominance: As space becomes a critical domain for military operations, control of the electromagnetic spectrum in space is paramount. Satellites and space assets are vulnerable to EW attacks.

THE KEY COMPONENTS

Activities used in EW include electro-optical, infrared and radio frequency countermeasures; EM compatibility and deception; radio jamming, radar jamming and deception, and electronic (or anti-jamming) countermeasures; electronic masking, probing, reconnaissance and intelligence; electronic security; EW reprogramming; emissions control; spectrum management; and wartime backup modes (Army 2020a, i, v–x). Traditional electronic warfare has three main components:

Electronic attack (EA)

Electronic attack (EA) is that branch of electronic warfare "involving the use of electromagnetic energy, directed energy, or antiradiation weapons to attack personnel, facilities, or equipment with the intent of degrading, neutralizing, or destroying enemy combat capability and is considered a form of fires " (Army 2016). Electronic attack uses point electromagnetic jamming, barrage jamming and sweeping, using electromagnetic deception techniques such as false targeting or generating duplicate targets.

Electronic attack, also known as electronic countermeasures (ECM), involves the offensive use of electromagnetic energy, directed energy, or anti-radiation weapons to attack and disrupt the adversary by "jamming" on communications systems or radar. Anti-radiation weapons include missiles or bombs that target a specific signal (radio or radar) to destroy the broadcast system. The operational objectives of ECM are:

- Countering ESM and hostile communications systems.
- Entering false data hostile electronic systems.
- Destruction of hostile electronic warfare system.

Electronic countermeasures can be classified into electro-optical-infrared (CM EO-IR) countermeasures (laser jamming, smoke/aerosols, signature suppressors, decoys, pyrotechnics/pyrophoric products, high energy lasers or directed IR energy countermeasures) and radio frequency countermeasures (e.g. precision-guided or radio-controlled weapons, communications equipment and sensor systems).

For this, various specific techniques are used, which can be classified into active ECM and passive ECM. Active ECM involves degrading the effectiveness of enemy electronic warfare systems through the generation and transmission of electromagnetic energy, through noise jamming and deceptive jamming (Neri 1991).

Noise jamming injects jamming signals into the enemy's electronic system so that the target signal is masked or completely jammed by jamming. There are different techniques to generate interference (Butt and Jalil 2013), such as spot jamming focused on a very narrow frequency band, sweep jamming that sweeps the entire frequency, or barrage jamming which targets several frequencies simultaneously.

Deceptive jamming produces false target positions and velocities through pseudo-signals, manipulative, or imitative techniques (introducing EM radiation into enemy channels that mimics their own emission is called imitative deception) (Singh 1988). Manipulative techniques modify friendly electromagnetic radiation to deceive the adversary, by generating false targets, falsifying the frequency range, speed and angle (Martino 2012) (Butt and Jalil 2013). False target generation is used against radar, early warning, and ground control interception to confuse the enemy radar operator (Rahman 2019) who will not be able to distinguish between false targets and real targets (Brunt 1978). Spoofing range, speed, and angle exploits enemy monitoring vulnerabilities (Martino 2012).

Passive ECM uses confusion reflectors to deceive the enemy's electronic systems, by chemical means (the use of smoke and chemical agents such as aerosols (Rahman 2019)) or mechanical (the use of specially designed mechanical objects, such as "chaff" made of thin dielectric fibers covered with metal (Grant and Collins 1982).Offensive ECMs often take the form of jamming, while self-protective (defensive) include the use of blip enhancement and jamming of missile terminals.

In the case of radars, ECM strategies include radar jamming, target changes, and changing the electrical properties of the air through jamming techniques such as jamming and deception (Polmar 1979). Radio jamming or communication jamming disrupts communications by lowering the signal-to-noise ratio.

Electronic protection

Electronic protection (EP) is that "Division of electronic warfare involving actions taken to protect personnel, facilities, and equipment from any effects of friendly or enemy use of the electromagnetic spectrum that degrade, neutralize, or destroy friendly combat capability" (Army 2016).

Electronic protection, also known as electronic protection measure (EPM) in Europe, or electronic countermeasure (ECCM), focuses on protecting electronic systems against attack by defeating enemy jamming. This involves the use of encryption, frequency hopping and hardening techniques to protect critical systems, using spread spectrum technologies, the use of restricted frequency lists, emissions control (EMCON) and low observability technology (stealth) (Army 2020a) (Tsui 2022).

Electronic protection, also known as electronic countermeasures (ECCM), uses electronic warfare tactics (EWTR) and techniques built into the design of electronic equipment to annihilate enemy ECM involving jamming and deception techniques. The domains commonly exploited by ECCM are:

- *Spatial ECCM*, such as side lobe canceller, side lobe obturation, or the burning technique (Neri 1991)(Grant and Collins 1982).
- *Spectral* (frequency-based) *ECCMs*, such as the technique with low probability of interception, frequency agility, or Doppler filtering (Grant and Collins 1982)(Skolnik 2008).
- *Temporal ECCM* (time-dependent techniques), including pulse expansion-compression, radiofrequency pulse agility, dickefix, or constant false alarm rate (Grant and Collins 1982)(Skolnik 2008).
- *ECCM via radar network*, a combination of at least two or three radars that provide information to a central hub (Sharma, Sarma, and Mastorakis 2020).

Electronic support

Electronic warfare support (ES) is the "division of electronic warfare involving actions tasked by, or under direct control of, an operational commander to search for, intercept, identify, and locate or localize sources of intentional and unintentional radiated electromagnetic energy for the purpose of immediate threat recognition, targeting, planning and conduct of future operations" (Army 2016).

Features of ES (US Marine Corps 2016):

- It is used in times of peace, crisis and war, which helps build an EW/information database for planning and operations.
- Provides all-weather, day/night, long-range intelligence gathering capability.
- Exploits an enemy's electromagnetic emissions and can provide information about enemy capabilities and intentions.
- It is hidden and passive.
- It is a non-intrusive method of gathering information.

Electronic warfare support systems collect data and produce intelligence for (US Marine Corps 2016):

- Corroboration with other sources of intelligence.
- Direct EA operations.
- Self-protection measures.
- Weapon systems for physical destruction.
- Supporting EP efforts.
- Creation or modification of EW databases.
- Information Operations (IO) support activities.

Electronic warfare support (ES), through electronic support measures (ESM), involves the collection and analysis of electromagnetic signals emitted by adversaries to detect, intercept, identify, and/or locate sources of radiated electromagnetic energy. This provides information and situational awareness, aiding commanders in decision making. Electronic support measures aim for immediate threat recognition, an activity called intelligence, surveillance and reconnaissance (ISR) or intelligence, surveillance, target acquisition and reconnaissance (ISTAR) (Kjellén 2018). Signals intelligence (SIGINT), which partly overlaps with ES, analyzes and identifies transmissions from sources such as radio communications, mobile phones, radar or microwave communications (Kjellén 2018). SIGINT consists of electronic intelligence (ELINT - compile operational data) and communications intelligence (COMINT - adversary communication) and ESM receiver. ESM has a tactical purpose that requires immediate action, while SIGINT collects intelligence data for later or non-real-time analysis (Rahman 2019).

The key functions of ESM systems are: intercept, identify, analyze and locate hostile electromagnetic radiation sources for the purpose of reconnaissance and tactical force engagement, possibly through an electronic order of battle (EOB), including ECM and ECCM operations.

ESM measures the parameters of the incoming radar signal in the operating frequency range: pulse width, pulse repetition frequency, signal strength, arrival time, arrival direction, etc. (X. Li et al. 2018), being composed of: antennas, receivers, signal processor, transmitter library computer and display unit (Shankar and Mohan 2013). The ESM receptor has the greatest influence on the characteristics of the ESM system (Martino 2012)(Sharma, Sarma, and Mastorakis 2020).

Electronic support measures can provide initial detection or knowledge of foreign systems, a library of technical and operational data on the foreign systems, and tactical battle information in which to use that library (Polmar 1979).

Desirable characteristics of electromagnetic surveillance and collection equipment include:

- broad spectrum or bandwidth capability, as foreign frequencies are initially unknown,
- wide dynamic range, because the signal strength is initially unknown,
- narrow bandpass to discriminate the signal of interest from other electromagnetic radiation at close frequencies, and
- good flight angle measurement to locate the transmitter (Polmar 1979).

Usually, several receivers are required to monitor the entire spectrum.

TECHNIQUES AND TACTICS

The main activities used in EW include the following (Army 2020a): countermeasures, EM battle management (EMBM), EM compatibility; EM fraud; EM hardening, EM interference resolution, EM intrusion, EM jamming, EMP, EM spectrum control, electronic intelligence gathering, electronic cloaking, electronic probing, electronic reconnaissance, electronic security, EW reprogramming, emission control, JEMSO, JEMSMO, low observability/stealth, signal interception and retransmission, wartime navigation (NAVWAR), precision geolocation, and wartime backup modes.

EW includes a number of techniques and tactics, such as (Duke 2023): jamming, spoofing, directed energy (DE), cyber electronic warfare (CEW), and electronic deception.

- **Jamming**: The deliberate radiation of EM to prevent or reduce the effective use of EMS by an enemy (Army 2020a).
- **Falsification**: Transmitting false information to an adversary's sensors or communications systems, causing confusion and potentially causing them to make incorrect decisions (Army 2020a, I–10).

- **Directed energy**: Is "an umbrella term covering technologies that relate to the production of a beam of concentrated electromagnetic energy or atomic or subatomic particles" (Army 2016). A directed energy weapon uses directed energy primarily "to incapacitate, damage, or destroy enemy equipment, facilities, and/or personnel" (Army 2016). Directed energy uses technologies that produce concentrated EM energy and atomic or subatomic particles as a means to incapacitate, damage, disable, or destroy enemy equipment, facilities, and/or personnel.
- **Electronic cyber warfare**: Combines cyberspace capabilities with traditional EW methods by infiltrating an adversary's computer or communications systems to steal or manipulate information and disrupt its operations (Yasar, Yasar, and Topcu 2012).
- **Electronic deception**: Using electronic means to mislead an adversary into believing something untrue, through techniques such as creating false targets on radar screens, using electro-optical, infrared, or radio frequency countermeasures, and transmitting false signals to confuse the adversary's sensors (Adamy 2001).
- **Anti-radiation weapons**: Use the radiated energy emitted by the target as a guidance mechanism to a targeted emitter (e.g. the high-speed anti-radiation missile [HARM] system).

Spectrum management includes "planning, coordinating, and managing use of the electromagnetic spectrum through operational, engineering, and administrative procedures". The objective of spectrum management is to enable electronic systems to perform their functions in their intended environment without causing or suffering unacceptable interference (Army 2016).

EW is used to create decisive, autonomous effects or to support military operations by generating various levels of control, detection, denial, deception, disruption, degradation, exploitation, protection and destruction.

- *In irregular warfare*, EW can influence the adversary, friendly population, and neutral population with the information operations (IO) message.
- *In information operations*, EW contributes by employing offensive and defensive tactics and techniques to shape, disrupt, and exploit adversary use of EMS while protecting friendly freedom of action.

- *In space operations*, physical maneuvers and uncontested EM collection involve some form of EW.
- *In cyberspace operations* it is necessary to use EMS to activate effects, by coordinating with EW.
- *In navigational warfare*, EW produces NAVWAR effects by influencing the transmission of global navigation satellite system or other radio signals.

Other techniques and tactics used in EW (Army 2020a):

- *Electromagnetic Battle Management (EMBM)*: Dynamic monitoring, assessment, planning and command of operations.
- *Electromagnetic Compatibility (EMC)*: The ability of systems, equipment and devices to function without suffering unacceptable degradation or causing unintended degradation.
- *Electromagnetic deception*: The deliberate radiation, reradiation, alteration, suppression, absorption, negation, enhancement, or reflection of EM energy in a manner intended to convey deceptive information to an enemy.
- *Electromagnetic hardening*: To protect against the unwanted effects of EM energy.
- *Electromagnetic interference resolution*: The process of systematically diagnosing the cause or source of EM interference.
- *Electromagnetic intrusion*: The intentional insertion of EM energy into transmission paths to deceive operators or cause confusion.
- *Electromagnetic jamming*: Altering EM energy to prevent or reduce the effective use of EMS by an enemy.
- *Electromagnetic Pulse (EMP)*: A powerful electronic pulse produced by a nuclear or conventionally generated explosion that produces surges.
- *Control of the electromagnetic spectrum*: Through the coordinated execution of JEMSO with other lethal and non-lethal operations affecting EMOE.
- *Electronic Intelligence (ELINT)*: A subcomponent of SIGINT
- *Electronic masking*: Controlled radiation of EM energy on friendly frequencies to shield emissions from friendly electronic communications systems
- *Electronic probing*: Intentional radiation designed to be introduced into the devices or systems of potential enemies.

- *Electronic reconnaissance*: Detection, location, identification and evaluation of foreign EM radiation.
- *Electronic security*: Protection against unauthorized persons in the interception and study of EM radiation.
- *Electronic warfare reprogramming*: Changing EW or target detection systems in response to validated changes in equipment, tactics, or EME.
- *Emission control*: Selective and controlled use of emitters to optimize C&C capabilities while minimizing detection by enemy sensors, mutual interference between friendly systems, and enemy interference.
- *Joint Electromagnetic Spectrum Operations (JEMSO)*: Coordinated efforts to exploit, attack, protect and manage EMOE to achieve objectives.
- *Joint Electromagnetic Spectrum Management Operations (JEMSMO)*: Planning, coordinating and managing the joint use of EMS through operational, engineering and administrative procedures.
- *Low observability/infiltration*: EP with low observability/stealth, to operate by reducing the possibility of detection by opponents.
- *Meaconing*: Receiving beacon signals and rebroadcasting them on the same frequency to confuse navigation
- *Naval Warfare (NAVWAR)*: Deliberate actions to secure and prevent specific naval intelligence.
- *Precision geolocation*: Planning, coordinating and managing friendly assets to geolocate enemy RF systems.
- *Wartime Standby Modes (WARM)*: Features and operating procedures that will contribute to military effectiveness if not known or misunderstood by opposing commanders prior to use, but could be exploited or neutralized if known in advance.

EW SYSTEMS

A typical configuration for an EW system depends on the particular application, but generally includes the following elements (Poisel 2008):

System control: Can be done with a single computer (centralized control) or multiple computers.

Antennas: Used to extract electromagnetic (EM) energy from the propagation medium, or to convert electrical energy into electromagnetic energy that can be propagated through the atmosphere.

Antennas convert electrical signals into propagating EM waves and vice versa, convert propagating EM waves into electrical signals. Typically, antennas for EW must be wideband, and have the same characteristics whether they are used for transmit or receive. The most important characteristics of antennas are frequency response (determines bandwidth), directionality (determines how an antenna focuses energy in certain directions), and impedance characteristics (to match that of the antenna). The most popular antenna types used for EW in the lower frequency ranges are dipole, monopole, and log periodic. As the frequencies of interest increase, other types of antennas are used.

Signal distribution: This is normally done at the output of the antennas and before the receivers.

Search receiver: Searches the frequency spectrum for signals of interest.

Connected receiver: For relatively long-term analysis of signals detected by other means.

Receivers for interception of communication signals depend on the type of signal to be intercepted. For narrowband signals, the most popular type of receiver was the superheterodyne. Where the instantaneous operating frequency of the transmitter is unknown, wideband receivers are required. The fundamental function of a receiver is to convert a signal from the antenna into a usable one, usually demodulated, by conversion and demodulation.

Signal processing: Detecting the presence of energy at a specified frequency and within a specified bandwidth, determining the modulation of a signal, and measuring the transmission speed of a digital communication signal.

Signal processing for direction finding: Locating the source of emitting communication signals, usually by triangulation.

Signal processing in EW involves processing signals to extract information from them.

Geolocation (fixation of position): Determining the location of an emitting target, based on temporal parameters associated with the input signal. Arrival time and/or arrival frequency difference or differential Doppler effect with two or more sensors by triangulation are used as methods.

Exciter: A high power amplifier, filters and an antenna, essentially a RF signal generator with the ability to modulate the generated signals.

Power amplifier: Amplifies the signal from the exciter.

Exciters and power amplifiers are included in an EW system when EA is called. The signals thus generated interfere with the adversary's communications. Most of the time it is necessary to inject more energy than the target emitter. The exciter generates the signal which is then increased in power by the power amplifier.

Filters: Limit the out-of-channel (unwanted) energy that the system emits.

Communications: The communications subsystem can be composed of several types of capabilities for command and control of the system.

Radar

"RADAR" is an acronym for RAdio Detection And Ranging, based on the reflection of electromagnetic waves. In 1903, the reflection of radio waves was used in Germany to demonstrate the detection of ships at sea. Practical development of pulse radar began in the 1930s, mainly in the United States, Great Britain and Germany. Radar can "see" further than the human eye and can more accurately assess the distance or range of an object. Radar systems must use target discriminators to isolate the desired target return: range, speed, and angle. The presence of an echo indicates target detection (* * * 2000).

Radar systems are designed to provide attack warning, target engagement information, and provide reasonably accurate target range, azimuth, and elevation information.

A radar transmits and receives electromagnetic radiation, called radio frequency (RF) radiation. The transmitted RF frequency affects the ability of a radar system to analyze the target, the ability of the transmitting antenna to focus the RF energy into a narrow beam, and the propagation of the signal through the atmosphere.

Each radar produces a radio frequency (RF) signal with specific characteristics that differentiate it from all other signals and define its capabilities and limitations. Pulse width (pulse duration), pulse repetition time (pulse repetition interval), pulse repetition frequency, and power are characteristics of the radar signal determined by the radar transmitter, providing a unique signature to identify a particular radar signal. Listening time, rest time and recovery time are the characteristics of the radar receiver. The individual components of a radar determine the capabilities and limitations of a particular radar system. The characteristics of these components also determine the countermeasures that will be effective against a particular radar system.

The primary purpose of radar systems is to determine the range, azimuth, elevation, or speed of a target. The ability of a radar system to determine and resolve these parameters depends on the characteristics of the transmitted radar signal.

The function of the antenna during transmission is to focus the radar energy from the transmitter into a patterned beam towards the desired direction. During reception or listening time, the function of the antenna is to collect the radar energy returning via the echo, transmitting these signals to the receiver. The method used by radar antennas to sample the environment is a critical design feature of the radar system. Radar horizon, direct terrain masking, and indirect terrain masking are limitations for all radar scans.

A target tracking radar (TTR) provides the information needed to guide a missile or aim a weapon to destroy a target. A typical TTR has individual tracking loops to track a target in range, azimuth, altitude, or speed. The TTR antenna is pointed at a single target. Once a target has been identified, the final stage of engagement is to guide a missile or projectile to destroy the target.

Radar jamming is the intentional radiation or re-radiation of radio frequency signals to interfere with the operation of a radar by saturating its receiver with false targets or false information about targets. The most commonly used types of radar jamming are noise and deception. The signal-to-noise ratio of the victim radar determines the vulnerability of the radar receiver to jamming, while the jamming-to-signal ratio is an indication of the ability of the jamming system to effectively jam the victim radar.

RELATIONSHIP OF EW TO OTHER COMBAT CAPABILITIES

Information and cyber warfare (Sfetcu 2023b): In the modern era, warfare extends into cyber space, where intelligence agencies play a vital role in defending against cyber threats. They actively monitor digital activities, identify potential cyber-attacks and assess the capabilities of hostile cyber actors. In addition, intelligence services engage in information warfare, countering enemy propaganda and influencing public perception to gain power in conflict. One of the significant challenges in the Russian-Ukrainian war was the widespread use of disinformation campaigns by both Russia and Ukraine. Disinformation and propaganda were used to sway public opinion, manipulate perceptions, and create confusion in enemy ranks. Intelligence services are forced to adapt and invest in combating disinformation, while ensuring the credibility and accuracy of their own reports.

Cyber warfare (Sfetcu 2023b) has been a component of the confrontation between Russia and Ukraine since the collapse of the Soviet Union in 1991. While the first attacks on the information systems of private enterprises and state institutions in Ukraine were recorded during the mass protests in 2013, the Russian cyber weapon Uroburos has existed since

2005. Russian cyber warfare continued with the penetration of Ukraine's power grid in 2015 at Christmas, and again in 2016 by paralyzing the State Treasury of Ukraine in December 2016, a massive hacker attack in June 2017 and attacks on Ukrainian government websites in January 2022.

Psychological warfare (Sfetcu 2023b): Intelligence activity can also play a role in psychological warfare, where the dissemination of carefully crafted information can influence enemy morale and decision-making. By strategically disseminating certain information or disinformation, intelligence services can create confusion, mistrust, and uncertainty among opposing forces, potentially undermining their resolve and cohesion.

In the last century, and especially in the second half, EW joined other combat capabilities and became one of the major competencies of war. The five core competencies together, PSYOP, CNO, EW, MILDEC, and OPSEC, are critical to shaping the information environment (Army 2020a, II–1).

Computer Network Operations (CNO) and EW: The more integrated EW and CNO are, the easier it is to collect, manipulate and disseminate information, as there is an increasing reliance on the EM spectrum in the use of computer networks, especially wireless networks.

The US defines a computer network attack (CNA) as including operations to disrupt, deny, degrade, or destroy information residing in computer and computer networks, or the computers and networks themselves (Army 2020a). There are potential benefits in a realignment of CNW terminology, doctrine, and even systems, with lessons learned from electronic warfare (R. Smith and Knight 2005).

Military Deception (MILDEC) and EW: Military deception consists of those "actions executed to deliberately mislead adversary military decision makers as to friendly military capabilities, intentions, and operations, thereby causing the adversary to take specific actions (or inactions) that will contribute to the accomplishment of the friendly mission" (Army 1996, I–1). This relationship is growing as militaries increasingly use the EM spectrum for deception purposes.

Operations Security (OPSEC) and EW: Operations security is the process of identifying critical information and denying it to adversary decision makers to cause them to miscalculate friendly forces, courses of action, and intentions (Army 2020a, II–3). Military missions that can avoid detection by enemy radar usually prove to be more effective. ES provides OPSEC with information on adversary capabilities and intentions to collect intelligence on friendly intelligence essentials via the EM spectrum. In a military deception campaign, electromagnetic deception and OPSEC must be integrated, synchronized, and coordinated.

Psychological Operations (PSYOP) and EW: Influencing the adversary must always be the ultimate objective of information operations.

Recent technological advances allow capabilities such as PSYOP and MILDEC to provide a greater number of enhanced capabilities, requiring greater EW involvement in these areas. EW aids PSYOP by degrading the enemy's ability to observe activities in theater, report those activities, and make decisions accordingly (Kucukozyigit 2006).

The supporting competencies of the IO are physical security, physical attack, counterintelligence (CI), information assurance (IA) and the combat camera (COMCAM), which directly or indirectly contribute to the effectiveness of the IO.

Physical security and EW: Using a jamming device for military convoys can be considered physical security. Physical security measures are used wherever EW equipment is present (Army 2020a, B-2).

Physical attack and EW: Physical attack disrupts, destroys, or damages targets of any kind using destructive kinetic power, providing an effective means of attacking adversary EW systems and thereby supporting the superiority of friendly EW operations.

Counterintelligence (CI) and EW: CI is comprised of information collected and activities conducted to counter adversary intelligence, espionage, sabotage, assassination, etc. (Army 2020a, II–7). CI supports EP and ES by providing electronic countermeasures (Army 2020a, B-3), and EW assets can be used to destroy or degrade enemy intelligence capabilities. Electronic intelligence collected through SIGINT and ES capabilities is used to assess, analyze, and update enemy intelligence capabilities.

Counterintelligence measures aim to prevent adversaries from infiltrating and gathering sensitive information from friendly forces. This is critical to maintaining operational security and ensuring that one's strategies and tactics remain confidential. Intelligence services monitor the protection of sensitive information and military operations from being compromised by hostile agents. Identifying and neutralizing enemy spies can have a significant impact on the enemy's ability to gather intelligence and disrupt their plans. The Russian-Ukrainian war is characterized by Russia's widespread use of disinformation and hybrid warfare tactics. Intelligence services play a critical role in detecting and countering these efforts. They monitor social media, online forums and traditional media to identify false narratives and propaganda spread by hostile actors. False information is used to provoke public outrage during wartime. In April 2014, Russian news channels *Russia-1* and *NTV* showed a man saying he was attacked by a fascist Ukrainian gang on one channel, and on the other channel saying they were funding the formation of anti-Russian right-wing radicals. In May 2014, Russia-1 aired a story about Ukrainian atrocities using footage from a 2012 Russian operation in the North Caucasus. In the same month, the Russian news network *Life* featured a photo from 2013 of an injured children in Syria as a victim of Ukrainian troops who had just recaptured

Donetsk International Airport. By understanding the disinformation landscape, intelligence services can inform governments and the public about the deceptive tactics used by Russia, ensuring that disinformation does not influence public opinion or compromise national authorities (Sfetcu 2023b).

Combat Camera (COMCAM) and EW: COMCAM provides leaders with imagery to support operational and planning requirements (Army 2020a, II–7). Intelligence-supporting ES capabilities also contribute to COMCAM's mission across the conflict spectrum. COMCAM can be used to assess the effectiveness of EW targeting, and EP contributes to the COMCAM mission by securely transmitting COMCAM images.

Information Assurance (IA) and EW: IA is comprised of measures that protect and defend information and information systems. EW provides operational protection against adversary and intelligence efforts targeting friendly electronic information and information systems (Army 2020a, II–6), and supports AI by protecting information, information systems, and assets (Army 2020a, B-3).

Cyber electronic warfare

In the early 2000s, cyber warfare began to emerge as a new concept. Its advantages were confirmed in the second Gulf War, in Estonia in 2007 when it was exposed to a cyber-attack by Russia (Dunn Cavelty 2012), and in Georgia during the South Ossetia war in 2008 (Yasar, Yasar, and Topcu 2012).

Cyber warfare involves the use of cyber-attacks at the state level, causing damage comparable to real warfare and/or disrupting enemy infrastructure and systems (Singer and Friedman 2014).

Taddeo offered the following definition of cyber warfare in 2012:

"[Cyber] Warfare is [the warfare grounded on certain] uses of ICTs within an offensive or defensive military strategy endorsed by a state and aiming at the immediate disruption or control of the enemy's resources, and which is waged within the informational environment, with agents and targets ranging both on the physical and non-physical domains and whose level of violence may vary upon circumstances." (Taddeo 2012)

Cyber security and cyber warfare have become critical issues in an increasingly interconnected world. Cybersecurity (the practice of safeguarding digital systems and data from malicious activity) is inextricably linked to cyberwarfare, which involves the use of digital technologies to disrupt, damage, or gain control over adversary computer systems. The line between these two fields is blurred, as cyber security strategies often have dual use as applications in cyber warfare and vice versa.

Cyber security and cyber warfare are intertwined in a complex relationship that shapes our digital world. As cyber threats continue to evolve, and nation-states engage in offensive cyber actions, the need for robust cyber security measures and international cooperation is more critical than ever. To effectively navigate this complicated nexus, stakeholders must continually adapt to the dynamic nature of the cyber domain, recognizing that digital warfare is as important as any physical battlefield in the 21st century.

In the digital age, the threat landscape is constantly evolving, requiring adaptive cybersecurity measures. Cyber threats encompass a wide range of activities, including data theft, malware attacks, denial-of-service attacks, and social engineering. These threats can target individuals, organizations or even entire nations. As cyber threats grow in complexity, so does the challenge of securing critical infrastructure and sensitive information.

The relationship between CW and EW can be thought of as the relationship between asymmetric and symmetric warfare. CW and EW were used together for the first time in the war between Russia and Georgia in 2008 (Yasar, Yasar, and Topcu 2012).

While electronic warfare uses the electromagnetic spectrum and CW uses elements of cyberspace, cyber electronic warfare proposes the integration of these two combat capabilities. The advantage of CEW is that while electronic attack can be detected, cyber electronic attack is almost impossible to detect.

Yasar, Yasar, and Topcu do a SWOT analysis of CEW, concluding that although it is technologically feasible to apply the CEW concept in an attack, there are some challenges, such as the complexity of the system of threats, the need to call on intelligence, and the use of different types of firewalls and passwords (Yasar, Yasar, and Topcu 2012).

Internet of Military Objects (IoMT)

The Internet of Military Things (IoMT) is a complex network of interconnected entities, or "things" with recognized benefits (Silicon Labs 2013), that communicate with each other to coordinate, learn, and interact with the environment for a wide range of activities in a more efficient and informed (Rowlands 2017) (Cameron 2018). The basic idea is that future military battles will be dominated by machine intelligence and cyber warfare (Kott, Alberts, and Wang 2015).

The devices ("objects") in the IoMT possess intelligent physical capabilities for sensing, learning and acting through integrated virtual or cyber interfaces (Kott 2018). In general, IoMT devices form a "data fabric"

(Sydney J. Freedberg Jr 2020) for data transport, data capture, sensing and actuation, and an overall device with processing and communication capabilities that can exchange information with the larger network (Russell and Abdelzaher 2018). The possibility of incorporating inanimate objects, such as plants and rocks, into the system by equipping them with sensors that will transform them into information collection points has also been suggested (Parker 2018) (e-Plants(Saxena 2017)).

THE MAIN COMPETITORS

The main competitors identified by the US in the 2022 National Defense Strategy are China and Russia. They, noting that the disruption of C&C systems could be a cost-effective solution for diminishing US military advantages (Hoehn 2021), focused on the development of EW systems for an informational dominance (Copp 2021).

US

Electronic warfare is defined by the US Department of Defense (DoD) as "military activities that use electromagnetic energy to control the electromagnetic spectrum (the 'spectrum') and attack an enemy" (CRS 2022).

The US National Defense Strategy, released in 2022, highlights efforts by China and Russia to modernize their forces to counter US military advantages. The Commission on National Defense Strategy stated that the United States is losing its edge in electronic warfare, recommending increased EW investments and the development of new concepts. The Army plans to invest in both airborne and ground-based EW programs through the acquisition of long-endurance, unmanned aerial EW systems and unit-level training. The Navy continues to support and upgrade its radio battalions designed for signature intelligence and electronic warfare, develops the Naval Integrated Fire Control-Counter Air (NIFC-CA) concept to help air counter adversaries in impossible or degraded environments, and funds the project Next Generation Jammer (CRS 2022).

The DOD EW Executive Committee, chaired by the Assistant Secretary of Defense, is tasked with "synchronizing and integrating EW across DOD components by sharing tactics, techniques, procedures, and technologies" (CRS 2022) and establishing DOD EW policy. The FY2019 National Defense Authorization Act included the creation of a cross-functional team for electromagnetic spectrum operations. The Electromagnetic Spectrum Supremacy Strategy was published on October 29, 2020.

The United States Joint All Domain Command and Control operational concept (JADC2) seeks to rapidly "sense," "understand," and "act" on information in the battlespace through the use of automation, artificial intelligence, predictive analytics, and machine learning (ML) (DoD 2022). The US perspective, focused on optimizing operations, neglects the additional focus on conflicting systems. EW is the essential condition of the successful implementation of JADC2.

By combining EW mechanisms with MILDEC 44 operations, the US can create chaos for adversary systems by injecting overwhelming amounts of signals and data, but at the risk of creating additional chaos for friendly forces. But controlled chaos is believed to be the solution to fool high-fidelity, advanced, and emerging threats (Duke 2023).

The Army's Electronic Warfare Planning and Management Tool (EWPMT) allows a commander to better understand and visualize the electromagnetic spectrum on the battlefield during an operation (Northrop 2022).

The Army has developed two systems called Terrestrial Layer Systems that will provide integrated electronic warfare and cyber capabilities on the battlefield.

The TLS-Brigade Combat Team program will provide Soldiers with integrated electronic warfare, cyber and signals intelligence capabilities at the brigade level.

In 2021, Northrop Grumman Corporation delivered one of the most advanced multi-purpose sensors, Arrays at Commercial Timescales - Integration and Validation (ACT-IV), which is based on an advanced electronically scanned active digital multi-purpose array (AESA).

Through the Multi-Function Electronic Warfare-Air Large (MFEW-AL) program, the US Army prepares for multi-domain operations and considers the long distances of the Pacific.

The Army is to pay special attention to electronic warfare and drone swarms through EDGE 22. The Army also plans to experiment with multi-intelligence detection capabilities.

SEWIP is the Navy's overall program to incorporate various EW capabilities into its ships using versions of the SLQ-32, the capability associated with SEWIP (Northrop 2022).

Actions within a potential EW (Army 2020a):

- *Organization for joint electronic warfare*: EW planning and operations can be shared among multiple branches of a joint staff; the EW staff of the commander of the joint electronic warfare force (JCEWS) is headed by an electronic warfare command officer. JCEWS develops operational plans (OPLAN) and concept plans and monitors routine EW operations and activities.

- *Electronic warfare intelligence support organization*: Each geographic commander must establish a frequency management structure that includes a joint frequency management office (JFMO) and establish procedures to support planned and ongoing operations. The Army is organized to work in an Electronic Warfare Task Force structure with the establishment of the EWO, EW Technician and EW Specialist Center Group comprising the Electronic Warfare Coordination Cell (EWCC). Marine EW assets are an integral part of the Maritime Air-Ground Task Force (MAGTF).
- *Multinational aspects of electronic warfare*: US planners should integrate US and partner nation EW capabilities into an overall EW plan, providing partner nations with information on US EW capabilities and partner nation EW assistance.

The national security of the United States is now dependent on large technology companies, which have a strong influence on policy makers (Henney 2019). They have the most talented people and hold the rights to the most powerful weapons (Kolhatkar 2019).

China

In 2021, China made public a new operational concept called Multidomain Precision Warfare (Insinna 2022) in response to JADC2. While similar to the US strategy, it places more emphasis on identifying adversary vulnerabilities through AI through kinetic and non-kinetic measures. China emphasizes targeting vulnerabilities in emerging US technologies.

China's AI strategy was covered by Elsa Kania, deputy senior fellow for technology and national security at the Center for a New American Security.

"China has made no secret of its goal to lead the world in AI, and the military, in particular, has seen greater progress than expected. This includes a long list of applications such as suicide drones, autonomous weapon systems, EW, cyber operations, wargaming, data analytics and situational awareness." (Friedrich 2020).

In July 2017, China's State Council launched an artificial intelligence plan and strategy to become the world leader in artificial intelligence by 2030, committing $150 billion to this goal (Baker 2018). By the end of 2019, China had reached its goal earlier than expected (G. C. Allen 2019). An advantage of China's strategy was the development of new innovative systems (Rogosa 2015). Thus, China possesses the sophistication and resources to hack network systems, establish footholds behind perimeter defenses, exfiltrate valuable information, and sabotage critical network functions (Carlin 2016). As of 2019, China is the world leader in missile technology with the development of deep reinforcement learning control systems for targeting and guidance (You, Diao, and Gao 2019) (Haney 2019).

Chinese arms manufacturers are already selling armed AI-controlled drones (G. C. Allen 2019), with Chinese companies developing AI working in cooperation with the Chinese military. It should be noted that China's development of increasingly autonomous robotic weapons and surveillance AI technology runs counter to China's stated goals of avoiding an AI arms race (Haney 2019).

Russia

In December 2010, the Russian military was equipped with its first multifunctional electronic warfare system (*Borisoglebsk 2*), mounted on nine MT-LB armored vehicles and used to suppress mobile satellite communications and satellite navigation signals (ODIN 2023).

According to a 2017 report by the International Center for Defense and Security, Russia's EW portfolio is geared towards NATO communications, radars, unmanned aerial vehicles and other provocative sensors (Northrop 2022).

According to Margarita Konaev of the Center for Security and Emerging Technology,

"Russia trails China and the U.S. in all metrics of AI. However, its military is leading the country's efforts to catch up in key areas, most of which involve military applications." Konaev listed three of Russia's investment focuses: military robotics and unmanned systems, electronic warfare (EW) capabilities and information warfare. Noting the country's quick pace when it comes to experimentation... They're quick to test, and they learn limitations under operational conditions." (Friedrich 2020)

According to Jonas Kjellen (Kjellén 2018), the modern Russian equivalent of EW was named, chronologically, as Radio Countermeasures (*Radioprotivodeistvie*, *RPD*), Enemy Radioelectronic Countermeasures Equipment (*Borba s radioelektronnymi sredstami przybna*, *BRESP*), and *Radioelektronnaia borba* (*REB*) starting from the 1960s (Liubin 2009). According to the Soviet Military Encyclopedia of 1984, electronic warfare is a set of measures taken for the identification and subsequent use of radioelectronic suppression on enemy radio-electronic equipment and systems and to protect the radio-electronic equipment and systems of one's own forces (* * * 1984, 615). Soviet EW was divided into offensive EW measures ("radioelectronic suppression", *Radioelektronnoe podavlenie*) and defensive: "radioelectronic suppression" (radioelectronic protection", *Radioelektronnaia zashchita*).

Since 1990, the definition of EW has undergone some changes; electronic warfare is a set of measures and actions — interconnected in time and by targets and tasks — taken by troops (forces) to detect enemy radio-electronic equipment and systems and ensure their subsequent destruction (using any type of weapon), elimination (removal from combat) or radioelectronic suppression, as well as radioelectronic protection of equipment and radioelectronic systems belonging to the forces; electronic warfare is a combat support function (* * * 1990, 357).

According to newer documents (Guzenko and Moraresku 2017, 14–16), electronic warfare is a set of activities and coordinated actions that include radio-electronic attack on enemy radio-electronic and technical-informational objects, radio-electronic protection of radio-electronic and technical-informational objects, countermeasures against technical reconnaissance and radioelectronic information support measures. Two new areas appear in the new definition, countermeasures against reconnaissance and technical information and support measures for radioelectronic information. Thus, the components of modern Russian electronic warfare are:

1. *Electronic attack*, including destructive EW weapons (Lakhin and Korobeinikov 2016), using functional attack, electronic countermeasures, anti-radiation missiles, and electronic simulation and imitation.

2. *Electronic protection*, as measures to ensure the functionality of radioelectronic equipment in a blocked environment (Kolesov and Nasenkov 2015, 17), including electronic hardening (increasing electronic resistance to various types of electromagnetic radiation) and electromagnetic compatibility to reduce harmful interference.

3. *Countermeasures* against technical reconnaissance (*protivodeistvie tekhnicheskim sredstam razvedki, PD TSR*) to protect against foreign reconnaissance (Krylov, Larionova, and Nikitina 2017, 74).

4. Radioelectronic information *support measures* for the support of the above three, including through comprehensive technical control (Krylov, Larionova, and Nikitina 2017, 165).

The role of EW is now much broader and introduces a larger set of means, including the use of anti-radiation missiles, DEW and cyber capabilities, with contemporary Russian EW possessing capabilities not only to temporarily suppress an adversary's electronic system, but also to inflict permanent damage.

In 2002, President Vladimir Putin signed a long-term EW policy and strategy document, *Osnovy politiki Rossiiskoi Federatsii v oblasti razvitiia sistemy radioelektronnoi borby na period do 2010 goda i dalneishuiu perspektivu* (Fundamental policies for the development of the Russian Federation and up to the system of electronic warfare by 2010). In February 2012, this strategy document was renewed. being valid "until 2020 and beyond" (Doskalov 2013). The five main directions of the new strategy document are: improving state control over the operation and development of EW; integration of the military EW domain with other domains for national security; exploitation of achievements in research and development for a new generation of EW systems; further development of the educational and scientific research EW system; and expanding military-technical cooperation and increasing the export potential of EW systems (Doskalov 2013) (Kjellén 2018).

Some experts note that Russian EW weapons are superior to American ones in several respects (Kube 2018). Russia is believed to be so focused on EW as a relatively inexpensive way to diminish an adversary's capabilities, in an effort to " asymmetrically challenge the Alliance on Russia's periphery and maximise its chances of success in any operation against NATO's eastern members." (McDermott 2017). Russia believes that EW assets could double the combat potential of ground forces, reducing air force losses by six times and naval losses by three times 25, EW thus acting as a powerful asymmetric tool. Also, the deterrent value of EW could persuade enemies not to engage in combat against Russia (P. Smith 2022).

Ukraine has provided a testing ground for Russian-developed EW capabilities, and the Syrian conflict zone has been described as "the most aggressive EW environment on the planet" by General Raymond Thomas, former commander of the US Special Operations Command (Clark 2018). An assessment by Alan Shaffer, assistant undersecretary for defense acquisition and sustainment, claims that the US has "lost the electromagnetic spectrum" (Freedberg 2014), and William Conley, former director of US EW, noted that it got here because of " 25 years of inattention" and that "we will get out of it with 25 years of attention." (Freedberg 2017)

Russia's intention is to have a larger share of the world market for military EW systems. But today's Russian EW industry also faces a number of challenges, such as attracting talented young people, creating EW industrial clusters, and the Ukrainian export embargo and Western sanctions (Kjellén 2018).

NATO

NATO has a comprehensive approach to EW. In October 1956, the Military Committee approved MC 0064, NATO Electronic Warfare Policy. The alliance later developed the NATO Electronic Warfare Task Force and then NATO Electronic Warfare L (NATO 2023). A 2007 document, MCM_0142 Nov 2007 Military Committee Transformation Concept for Future NATO Electronic Warfare, recognized EME as an operational maneuver space/domain and battle environment/domain.

Between November 25-27, 2019, the NATO Electronic Warfare Advisory Committee (NEWAC) convened its 107th plenary meeting at NATO headquarters in Brussels. NATO EMS Strategy, the recognition of EW as a training discipline and the improvement of NATO EW policy and concept for the future of EW were discussed. Colonel Kabasakal emphasized the importance of this strategy for NATO, "the need for military forces to have unimpeded access to and use of the electromagnetic environment is essential to the success of most military operations. It will also determine the efficiency of our counter-measures in the Electronic Warfare domain and our ability to protect our capabilities and troops" (NATO 2019). The NATO Electromagnetic Operations (NEMO) conducted in October was given as an example.

NATO has adopted simplified language similar to that used in other combat environments (sea, land, air/space), retaining the traditional terms for electronic countermeasures (ECM), electronic protection measures (EPM) and electronic support measures (ESM) . According to NATO, other EM operations include intelligence, surveillance, target acquisition and reconnaissance (ISTAR) and signals intelligence (SIGINT).

The NATO Electromagnetic Warfare Advisory Committee (NEWAC), established in 1966, is the main forum within NATO for consultation and coordination on EW matters. This committee advises and implements the policies of the Military Committee, NATO's senior military authority that advises the North Atlantic Council. NEWAC consists of two working groups: the NATO Electromagnetic Warfare Working Group (NEWWG), and the NATO Emitter Database Advisory Group (NEDBAG) (NATO 2023).

NATO's Joint Electronic Warfare Staff (JEWCS) is a multinational military unit for EW expertise, support and training. The Electronic Warfare Liaison Committee (NEWLC) coordinates EW policy, equipment, training and publications among Allies (NATO 2023).

NATO now uses the term "electromagnetic warfare" to more precisely identify the importance of the electromagnetic spectrum in EW. NATO EW policy continues to be covered by MC 0064 (NATO 2023).

European Union

The Capability Development Plan (CDP) remains the main reference for European Union defense planners. "Europe's future security depends on a more robust and agile response. By working together to develop stronger and more credible military capabilities, the EU can be proactive in safeguarding its security, asserting its autonomy, and ensuring the safety and well-being of its citizens. This will require a deep commitment to collaboration and innovation, as well as a willingness to embrace new technologies," said Jin Sedivy, Executive Director of EDA (European Defence Agency 2023).

According to CDP, an approach based on integrated multi-domain collaborative systems is considered the most appropriate strategy to counter emerging threats. Cyber threats and electronic warfare systems are considered the biggest threats, along with the use of drone swarms. The electromagnetic environment is expected to become more congested, and the related infrastructure will be even more critical due to the huge increase in data management and communication needs. Consequently, the freedom to use the electromagnetic spectrum will become a challenge, along with electronic warfare, cyber situational awareness, and network resilience. Electromagnetic Spectrum Operations (EMSO) will play a major role to achieve dominance of the electromagnetic spectrum. Technological developments that enable an advantage over the adversary in the electromagnetic spectrum will be essential to meet the threats of electronic warfare. Cognitive superiority and artificial intelligence technologies can improve operations in the electromagnetic spectrum (European Defence Agency 2023).

Intercepting hypersonic weapons and ballistic missile attacks requires integrated and layered defense systems using non-kinetic systems, including electronic warfare systems, directed energy weapons or electromagnetic pulses, especially in saturation attacks.

Regarding the Internet of Things (IoT), the main concern is cybersecurity due to vulnerabilities to cyber-attacks, and the need for high-capacity wireless networks will require a better protected use of the electromagnetic spectrum.

Autonomous systems can be used in electronic warfare tasks to protect military assets by detecting and neutralizing electromagnetic spectrum threats and for offensive actions such as jamming.

New materials and fabrication techniques (new metals, synthetic biology, nanotechnology, stealth design, etc.) will influence advanced communication capabilities in the electromagnetic spectrum, and metamaterial-based antennas will increase output power, improve directionality, and extend the range of frequency, making them useful in both offensive and defensive electronic warfare.

According to the European Defense Agency,

"Electronic warfare and cyber offensive means will play a major role in controlling the heavily congested electromagnetic spectrum of future battlefields, which will be critical to achieve military superiority. The development of enhanced and inexpensive sensors will significantly improve electronic warfare systems, which will be a powerful effector against critical infrastructures, communication networks, platforms, and other critical assets. Likewise, cyber-attacks will be used to disrupt or degrade adversaries' assets remotely and even anonymously, which will bring several possibilities and challenges for military forces. Robotics and autonomous systems will be broadly integrated into military units, performing a great variety of functions in several missions. Autonomous platforms, manned-unmanned teaming, and the related adaptation of tactics will bring several challenges to force protection but will also present new opportunities to carry out missions with less risk to human life. Human enhancement could also be a disruptive factor for engagement capabilities. Technological developments in the fields of exoskeletons, wearable sensors, brain-computer interfaces, AI-driven systems, augmented and virtual reality devices (AR/VR), and synthetic biology devices will enable significant improvements to soldiers' physical and cognitive abilities." (European Defence Agency 2023)

CHALLENGES AND TRENDS

Electronic warfare was conceived a quarter of a century ago, developing through the exponential growth of space and cyber technologies that rely primarily on electromagnetic signals. But EME is an operational environment that must be configured to support EMO. The modern challenges of dealing with advanced adversary capabilities, particularly in confrontations requiring access and area denial operations, have brought EW back to the fore. NATO is currently rewriting its EW doctrine and investigating how to operate more effectively in EMS.

Soon, warfare will be characterized by advanced and intelligent threats operating in EMS. Thus, operational planners must consider the composition and balance of forces, and EW measures will become a necessity for information and communication systems in military operations (Duke 2023).

The main challenges and tensions derived from the specialty studies:

- *Spectrum congestion*: The proliferation of wireless technologies and IoT devices has led to increased spectrum congestion, making it more difficult to operate in the EM spectrum.
- *AI and machine learning*: Adversaries are incorporating artificial intelligence and machine learning into EW tactics, enabling more dynamic and adaptive electronic attacks.
- *Legal and ethical concerns*: The use of EW techniques in cyberspace raises legal and ethical questions, particularly regarding the protection of civilian infrastructure.

Electronic warfare has evolved significantly since its inception to become an integral part of modern military operations. To maintain a competitive advantage, the military must continuously adapt and innovate in this area. As technology continues to advance, the electronic warfare landscape will remain dynamic and emerging challenges will require a comprehensive and multifaceted approach. Continued research and development in the field of electronic warfare is essential to ensure national security and military effectiveness in an increasingly interconnected and contested world.

ASYMMETRIC WARFARE

Electronic warfare plays a crucial role in contemporary asymmetric warfare scenarios where technologically advanced militaries engage non-state actors or less advanced adversaries.

Asymmetric warfare, characterized by disparities in military capabilities between opposing forces, has become a defining feature of contemporary conflict. In such situations, the use of advanced technology, especially in the field of electronic warfare, has a profound impact on the outcome of conflicts. EW encompasses a wide range of activities involving the use of the electromagnetic spectrum to exploit, protect and control information and communications systems.

Electronic warfare systems, a very effective method of winning important victories or achieving operational successes, have not received enough attention for a long time. With the changing nature of security, the importance of electronic warfare systems has re-emerged, especially in unstable conflict situations, and states have made efforts to make rapid progress in this area for advantages in conflict zones in recent years. We are already in the period of fourth generation warfare and the threats are not only brought by ferocious military equipment, but states also especially use hybrid warfare and asymmetric warfare tactics to create pressure on adversaries. Electronic warfare systems are intensively used in hybrid and asymmetric warfare, becoming one of the key points of future security parameters. Developing countries with the desire to become a regional power place special emphasis on electronic warfare. Electronic warfare systems can no longer be ignored to ensure security and victory in future wars or conflict zones.

The emergence of AI, quantum computing, LAWS, hypersonic weapons, and DE systems require new and often asymmetric solutions in EMS.

Electronic countermeasures are a vital aspect of EW in asymmetric warfare. These involve actions taken to protect friendly forces from enemy electronic threats. In asymmetric conflicts, non-state actors or less advanced adversaries often rely on guerrilla tactics, hiding in urban environments or remote areas and using rudimentary electronic equipment.

Electronic support involves activities aimed at collecting, intercepting, and analyzing electronic signals. In asymmetric warfare, this can help identify and locate enemy positions, communication channels, and command structures. For example, unmanned aerial vehicles (UAVs) equipped with advanced electronic sensors can provide invaluable information on insurgent movements, aiding in precision strikes or targeted operations. The ability to gather electronic intelligence is a powerful tool that can mitigate the disadvantages of operating in unfamiliar and complex environments.

Electronic attack involves the use of electromagnetic energy to damage, disrupt or destroy an adversary's electronic systems. In asymmetric warfare, advanced militaries can use electronic attacks to degrade the enemy's ability to coordinate, communicate, and control its forces. This may involve the use of electronic warfare platforms or cyber operations to target an adversary's command and control infrastructure, thereby disrupting their ability to conduct effective operations.

Electronic warfare has a profound impact on the tactics and strategies used in asymmetric warfare. For advanced militaries, it provides an asymmetric advantage, allowing them to neutralize the technological limitations of their adversaries. They can operate in hostile environments with improved situational awareness, perform precise strikes and minimize collateral damage. However, non-state actors and less advanced adversaries have also adapted to the challenges posed by electronic warfare. They resorted to non-standard, low-tech methods of communication and sought refuge in areas where electronic warfare may have limited effectiveness.

The ongoing conflicts in the Middle East provide notable examples of electronic warfare in asymmetric warfare. Advanced militaries such as the United States and its allies have used electronic warfare to disrupt the communications networks of insurgent groups and locate high-value targets. On the other hand, non-state actors such as the Islamic State have adapted by using encrypted communication channels and low-tech tactics to evade surveillance and electronic attack.

The use of electronic warfare in asymmetric conflicts raises ethical concerns. The potential for collateral damage, invasion of privacy, and blurring of lines between combatants and non-combatants are all ethical dilemmas associated with EW. Striking the right balance between achieving military objectives and respecting human rights and international law is a complex challenge in the field of electronic warfare.

Electronic warfare is an indispensable component of modern asymmetric warfare. It significantly influences the tactics and strategies used by both technologically advanced armies.

2 ARTIFICIAL INTELLIGENCE

Artificial intelligence/machine learning (AI/ML) is a critical force multiplier in electronic warfare (EW) and can be a highly effective tool when applied in areas such as signal recognition, emission and signal control, emitter classification, threat recognition and jamming identification. From tactical situational awareness and management, threat recognition and classification, and emission and signature control tactics, to over-the-horizon targeting and non-kinetic sights using non-organic EW capabilities, AI/ML will be an enormous advantage in force lethality (Gannon 2023).

The AI/ML technique for EW integration is called Q-learning algorithms, a type of algorithmic reinforcement learning (H. Li et al. 2021). Most EW capabilities do not require complex models to integrate with AI/ML.

AI/ML can also improve the technique of "fingerprinting" transmitters by analyzing transmitter parameters and modulating the pulse from the transmitter. But these transmitter parameters often change over time or are switched between platforms, which is a challenge (Gannon 2023).

AI is generally defined as a computing system capable of superior human-level cognition. Current artificial intelligence systems are classified as "narrow AI," trained to perform specific tasks.

The application of artificial intelligence in conjunction with EW has the potential to bridge the gap between desired warfighting capability and acquired skills. AI is already considered essential for mobile EW systems deployed with battlefield formations (De Spiegeleire, Maas, and Sweijs 2017), due to AI's ability for effective decision support, handling large amounts of data, situational awareness, scenario visualization evolving and generating appropriate responses, and better self-control, self-regulation and self-action due to AI's inherent computational and decision-making capabilities (Gulhane 2018).

In EMS operations, the goal is to respond immediately. With AI and ML, the computer decides the next steps. Due to the unpredictable behavior of the system, even the people responsible for the system cannot predict its exact behavior. If a radar tries to track a jet, for example, the adversary's countermeasures can cause it to fail. Using ML, that radar will repeatedly try new approaches to achieve success (Friedrich 2020).

Modern AI systems are capable of processing information to make predictions and achieve goals (Tegmark 2018). As a result, these systems are transforming the foundations of the defense industry, national security, and global warfare.

Advantages and opportunities of integrating artificial intelligence in electronic warfare:

- Speed and efficiency:
    - The ability of AI to process large amounts of data in real time.
    - Enhanced decision-making capabilities for faster response in dynamic electronic environments.
- Precision and accuracy:
    - Improved targeting through AI-based analytics.
    - Collateral damage reduction through precise electronic warfare tactics.

THE HISTORICAL BACKGROUND OF ELECTRONIC WARFARE

In order to understand the current state of electronic warfare, a brief historical overview is necessary, which shows the increasing complexity of electronic threats and the need for advanced technologies to counter them.

According to the work *Evoluția inteligenței artificiale în domeniul securității naționale* (Sfetcu 2023a), in the late 1990s, the US Department of Defense developed plans for a "network-centric" war by integrating artificial intelligence (Day 2016). Examples of projects are Nett Warrior (formerly Ground Soldier System or Mounted Soldier System) (Magrassi 2002b) and Force XXI Battle Command Brigade (Magrassi 2002a).

In the 21st century, national security organizations are using artificial intelligence to help them find, according to Dan Coats in 2017, "innovative methods for using data to accelerate the pace and quality of analytic insight" (Coats 2021).

Around 2010 there was an explosion of interest in AI, due to the convergence of three favorable developments (Congressional Research Service 2020): (1) the availability of big data sources, (2) improvements in machine learning approaches , and (3) increasing processing power (Tang 2020). This led to the development of the weak form of AI, with algorithms for specific problems such as gaming, image recognition and navigation. Rapid advances in AI have sparked a wave of investment. Unclassified DoD (US) investment in AI has grown from just over $600 million in FY2016 to $2.5 billion in FY2021, with over 600 active AI projects (C. Smith 2019)(Congressional Research Service 2020).

In 2011, the Czech National Security Authority (NSA) was appointed as the national authority for the cyber agenda, with a special strategy for the integration of artificial intelligence and the defense of national security from this perspective (Kadlecová et al. 2020).

At the level of the European Union, the adoption of the Cybersecurity Strategy in 2013 by the European Commission (Kadlecová et al. 2020) boosted efforts to implement artificial intelligence. The EU finances various programs and institutions in this regard, such as Competence Research Innovation (CONCORDIA), which brings together 14 member states (Davenport and Kalakota 2019) and Cybersecurity for Europe (CSE) (CS Europe 2023), which brings together 43 partners involving 20 by member states. The European Network of Cyber Security Centers and Competence Center for Innovation and Operations (ECHO) (EMK 2023) brings together 30 partners from 15 member states, and SPARTA (SPARTA 2023) consists of 44 partners involving 14 member states.

In 2016, the U.S. Army Research Laboratory (ARL) created the Internet of Battlefield Things (IoBT) project to better integrate IoT technology into military operations (CRA 2017).

On July 20, 2017, the Chinese government launched a strategy to become the world leader in AI by 2030 (State Council 2017). In the same year, Vladimir Putin declared that "whoever becomes a leader in this field will rule the world." (Simonite 2017)

In 2017, ARL established the Internet of Battlefield Things Collaborative Research Alliance (IoBT-CRA) to advance the theoretical foundations of IoBT systems (Polit 2018). Also, DARPA (USA) has developed a program called Ocean of Things, for an awareness of the persistent maritime situation on large oceanic areas (MeriTalk 2018).

In 2018, the German government established a strategy for artificial intelligence, through a collaboration with the French, with tasks in cyber security. In Germany, artificial intelligence is addressed through cyber security, recognized as a government task with responsibilities divided among three ministries: Federal Ministry of the Interior, the Federal Ministry of Defense and the Federal Ministry of Foreign Affairs, and several institutions with specific objectives (Kadlecová et al. 2020).

The US National Defense Strategy, released in January 2018, identified artificial intelligence as one of the key technologies that " ensure we [the

United States] will be able to fight and win the wars of the future." (Department of Defense 2018) The US National Intelligence Directorate issued the AIM Initiative in 2019 (AIM 2019), a strategy designed to add intelligence with the help of machines, allowing intelligence services to process huge amounts of data faster than before and allow human intelligence officers to attend to other tasks. The US military has already integrated AI systems into combat through Project Maven, to identify insurgent targets in Iraq and Syria (Weisgerber 2017). In recent years, the US Department of Defense has initiated several projects based on IoMT and artificial intelligence, such as the Connected Soldier for smart personal equipment (Stackpole 2016).

In the UK the AI strategy is of particular relevance to all involved in Defense Force Development and Defense Transformation for an 'AI ready' system. The Defense Digital Strategy (2021) (Ministry of Defence 2021b) and the Defense Data Strategy (2021) (Ministry of Defence 2021a) have been implemented, creating a new digital AI hub. Some elements will be provided or supported by panDefence, based on an IA strategy note (Ministry of Defence 2022).

A prominent use of artificial intelligence by Ukraine in its conflict with Russia is the use of facial recognition software to spot Russian attackers and identify Ukrainians killed in the ongoing war (Tegler 2022). Putin recognizes the power and opportunities of weapons using AI, stating that artificial intelligence is the future of all mankind (Gigova 2017). After Russia invaded Ukraine on February 24, 2022, the Ukrainian military uses drones (BSI 2023) that can take off, land and navigate autonomously, and that can receive information collected by US surveillance operations on intelligence on the ground combat and national security about Russia (Tucker 2022). Russia, for its part, is using AI to analyze battlefield data from surveillance images.

The AI arms race is underway, mainly between the great powers (Gambrell and Isidro 2022). There is currently a global campaign to ban the killer robots, with a petition (Vincent 2017) to the United Nations calling for new regulations on the development and use of AI technologies (Sfetcu 2023a).

THE ROLE OF ARTIFICIAL INTELLIGENCE IN ELECTRONIC WARFARE

The inclusion of AI in EW systems makes them very effective as autonomous systems (J. Allen and Massolo 2020). For military applications, AI-supported data processing systems are already in use, and intelligent communication attributes have become indispensable (Liao, Li, and Yang

2018).

AI is already implemented through numerous applications in EW:

- *Signal intelligence and machine learning*: AI applications in signal processing for improved information gathering; machine learning algorithms for pattern recognition and anomaly detection in vast data sets.
- *Cyber operations and AI*: Using artificial intelligence for proactive cyber defense and response; autonomous cyber capabilities and their implications for offensive operations.
- *Electronic attack and AI*: Electronic attack strategies based on artificial intelligence to disrupt enemy communication system; adaptive and self-learning algorithms for real-time adjustments in electronic attack scenarios.

AI-based EW systems can be classified into EW systems that affect the operational level of warfare, and those that affect the strategic level. At the operational combat level AI can help in achieving tactical objectives, planning, eliminating uncertainty and effective preparation, such as (Sharma, Sarma, and Mastorakis 2020):

- Collecting, interpreting, and analyzing information (Davis 2019).
- In war games, increasing the power of simulations and game tools.
- In the case of unmanned vehicles such as UAVs for battlefield guidance, or in combination with robots for autonomous operation (Brooks 2018).

At the strategic level, AI can assist in organizing the order of battle, assigning forces, war strategies, decisions about scale and escalation, sharing and interpreting information, the scope and nature of war, the consequences of deploying assets, etc. (Sharma, Sarma, and Mastorakis 2020) Thus AI can be used in intelligence, surveillance and reconnaissance (ISR), targeting and navigation, or probing, mapping and hacking computer networks (Davis 2019). AI techniques can also be used in detecting RF signals from adversaries and predicting threats (Microwaves 2019).

Specific applications

ECM: ECMs are time- and location-dependent, and can be assisted by a wide range of ML/DL tools, such as the use of convolutional neural networks (CNNs) for radar jamming signal classification (Shao, Chen, and Wei 2020), detection and barrage jamming classification for synthetic aperture radar (SAR) based on CNN (Junfei et al. 2018), prediction of suitable jamming technique for a received threat signal using deep learning

(Lee, Jo, and Park 2020), or "chaff" in EW (Liu et al. 2017).

ECCM: Using frequency-agile (FA) radar in radar anti-jamming models with a reinforcement-based anti-jamming frequency hopping algorithm for cognitive radar (Kang et al. 2018), or using detectors to maintain a high probability detection and a low false alarm rate (Akhtar and Olsen 2018). The most used ML/DL techniques include (Sharma, Sarma, and Mastorakis 2020):

- *ANN*: A simplified mathematical analogue of the human neural network, used for the process of radar transmitter recognition and identification, jamming style selection, etc. (Petrov, Jordanov, and Roe 2013) Combined with other AI techniques can form hybrid algorithms for developing a jamming detection system, recognition of radar antenna scanning parameters, etc. (Wan et al. 2019)
- *CNN*: A type of DL with great advantages in extracting discriminative and static features of inputs, successfully applied in the field of radar jamming signal classification and radar signal processing (Shao, Chen, and Wei 2020).
- *Long short-term memory (LSTM)*: A modified architecture of RNN, capable of learning long-term dependencies (Goodfellow, Bengio, and Courville 2016), mainly used to solve the time prediction problem in radar signal processing and for predicting appropriate jamming techniques (Lee, Jo, and Park 2020).
- *Deep Reinforcement Learning (DRL)*: An area of machine learning used to take appropriate action to maximize reward in a given situation, used to find the best possible behavior or path that should be taken in a specific situation (Y. Li et al. 2019), especially in the development of anti-jamming algorithms for cognitive radar (Kang et al. 2018)

AI TECHNIQUES

Commonly used AI techniques are machine learning (ML), fuzzy systems, and genetic algorithms.

Machine learning

Artificial Neural Network (ANN) can be trained for pattern recognition, classification, data clustering, etc. through supervised or unsupervised learning. It is used for, among others, transmitter signal identification and classification, radar antenna scan parameter recognition, appropriate jamming style selection, etc. (Qiang, Wei-gang, and Yuan 2018).

Machine learning has found many uses in EW (Casterline et al. 2022):

- *Engaging agile threat emitters.* Adversary sensors and communications systems adapt quickly and operate across the entire EM spectrum. The Behavioral Learning for Adaptive Electronic Warfare (BLADE) program and the Adaptive Radar Countermeasures (ARC) program have been successful in overcoming these problems.

- *Broadband detection.* For real-time accurate situational awareness of the EM spectrum, ES sensors must observe multiple gigahertz of spectrum simultaneously. ML techniques can help eliminate low-priority detections faster in the processing chain.

- *Resources management.* EW resources must be balanced to effectively engage RF communications and radar targets. Bayesian probability theory allows us to represent units of evidence as real numbers that can be used to strengthen or eliminate competing hypotheses, providing significant capability advancement in resource management for EW planning and decision-making during EW operations.

Automatic Modulation Recognition (AMR) informed transmitter identification allows distinguishing between threat emissions and those that are friendly or neutral. Modern adaptation threats have driven the need for detection ML techniques that can rapidly recognize and characterize novel detections at machine speed.

- *Anomaly detection using learned features.* After learning a set of modulation features, they can be used for classification or anomaly detection.

Autonomous resource allocation provides a useful means of mapping observed RF data into emitters of specific observed adverse threats.

- *Resource allocation problem.* One way to approach autonomous resource allocation is through Bayesian probability theory (Casterline et al. 2022).

Deep Neural Network (DNN) has better feature expression than ANN, and an ability to fit complex mapping. There are three commonly used DNN models: Deep Belief Networks (DBN), Stacked Autoencoder (SAE), and Deep Convolution Neural Networks (DCNN). It is used in EW systems for radar signal processing, emitter identification and classification, development of improved anti-jamming methods, detection of jamming and its characteristics, etc. (Elbir, Mishra, and Eldar 2019)

Fuzzy systems

Fuzzy logic allows tracking finite variations of inputs, fuzzy systems attempting to resemble human decision-making methodology (Hamilton, Jakeman, and Norton 2008), but without the learning or memory capacity. It is used in combination with other techniques to form hybrid systems for radar and related signal processing applications (Waghray and Menghal 2011).

Genetic algorithm

The genetic algorithm attempts to replicate naturally occurring evolutionary processes, an iterative technique based on probability. It is used in optimization problems, in combination ANN and DNN for several dynamic environments (Wei et al. 2019), including radar signal processing (Waghray and Menghal 2011).

TRENDS

Different artificial intelligence algorithms can be used through neuro-computing and deep learning techniques (Sharma, Sarma, and Mastorakis 2020):

- A learning algorithm is discussed by Amuru et al. (Amuru et al. 2015) to jam sender-receiver pairs in electronic warfare.
- A soft-computing model for threat detection in EW settings is discussed by Noh and Jeong (Noh and Jeong 2010).
- Fuzzy logic and neural networks for decision making in the EW environment are discussed in the article of Waghray and Menghal (Waghray and Menghal 2011).
- A radar signal pulse modulation recognition method based on convolutional denoising autoencoder and deep convolutional neural network (DCNN) is discussed by Qu et al. (Qu et al. 2019).
- An automatic modulation classification system for radar signals based on AI-based hybrid algorithm including Naive Bayesian and SVM is presented by Wang et al. (Wang et al. 2018).
- The performance of an anti-blocking method based on deep reinforcement learning (DRL) is discussed by Li et al. (Y. Li et al. 2019).

- A method based on deep learning is proposed by Elbir, Mishra, and Eldar (Elbir, Mishra, and Eldar 2019) to select antennas in a cognitive radar scenario.
- The artificial intelligence-based method presented by Gecgel Cetin, Goztepe, and Karabulut Kurt (Gecgel Cetin, Goztepe, and Karabulut Kurt 2019) can determine the presence of jamming, along with its attack characteristics.
- MASINT analyze target radar signatures (Dudczyk and Kawalec 2013), helps detect, track, identify and describe the distinctive characteristics of emitters.
- A radar signal recognition system based on non-negative matrix factorization network and ensemble learning is presented by Gao et al. (Gao et al. 2019).
- A radar transmitter signal identification and classification method based on clustering and probabilistic neural networks is discussed by Liao, Li, and Yang (Liao, Li, and Yang 2018).
- Petrov, Jordanov, and Roe (Petrov, Jordanov, and Roe 2013) present the ANN-based method for timely and reliable recognition of radar signal emitters.
- An automatic radar waveform recognition system for detecting, tracking, and locating radars with low probability of interception is discussed by Zhang et al. (Zhang et al. 2017).
- Another radar signal classification system based on neural networks is presented by Shao, Chen, and Wei (Shao, Chen, and Wei 2020).
- A method combining visibility graph with machine learning for radar antenna scan pattern recognition is discussed by Wan et al. (Wan et al. 2019).
- Another algorithm for radar antenna scan period (ASP) estimation and radar antenna scan type recognition in EW environment is presented by Barshan and Eravci (Barshan and Eravci 2012).
- An innovative framework for testing different CEW tasks, where the DRL algorithm was used for target search purposes, is discussed by You, Diao, and Gao (You, Diao, and Gao 2019).
- The short-range chaotic compound detection system is a system that has strong anti-jamming capability (Wei et al. 2019).
- A technique for extracting and analyzing various features of the decoy jammer and target echo signal to achieve anti-deception

jamming of short-range chaotic compound detection system is discussed by Wei et al. (Wei et al. 2019).

- The filtering method based on the network of stacked bidirectional recurrent units (SBiGRU) and infinite training is discussed by Chen et al. (Chen et al. 2019).

According to MarketsandMarkets (MarketsAndMarkets 2023), in June 2022, Lockheed Martin Corporation launched a new AI/ML solution with a cognitive mission manager and a suite of command and control services to provide timely and accurate operational intelligence, the Cognitive Tip & Cue product for finding tanks on the battlefield, detecting changes using satellite imagery, and TruthTrail, an app that features a simulated environment that "rewards" taggers for their work.

In July 2022, Raytheon Technologies used the C3 AI platform to provide next-generation artificial intelligence and machine learning capabilities with a rapid solution available for the US Army's Tactical Intelligence Targeting Access Node (TITAN) program.

In January 2023, Lockheed Martin Corporation unveiled its new Aegis AI model, used to improve the operational efficiency of the Agis Combat System for improved decision-making, situational awareness, reduced reaction time, and the ability to defend against hypersonic threats.

In March 2023, Northrop Grumman Corporation, together with Shield AI, was selected by the US Army for the Future Tactical Unmanned Aircraft System (FTUAS) competition, Increment 2, to replace the RQ-7B Shadow tactical unmanned aerial system (UAS) with advanced capabilities.

In April 2023, Raytheon Technologies Corporation launched an AI-assisted EO/IR system, RAIVEN, which enables military pilots to achieve faster and more accurate threat identification (MarketsAndMarkets 2023).

CHALLENGES AND RISKS

The Electromagnetic Spectrum Supremacy Strategy (ESSS), published in October 2020 by the US, addresses the many challenges faced in securing, maintaining access to, using, and maneuvering the electromagnetic spectrum (Gannon 2023).

The future of AI in EW is directly related to the ability to design autonomous systems with independent reasoning based on knowledge and expertise. Most military UAVs currently require significant human intervention to execute their missions. Current operational systems are more automated than autonomous, but there are significant global efforts in research and development of autonomous systems, although there are cost and organizational issues that limit the operational implementation of autonomous systems.

The future of warfare is related to AI, despite all the problems specific to the military establishment, such as the ability to develop and test safe and controllable autonomous systems and the lower attractiveness in the aerospace and defense sector due to lower funding compared to private industry.

Future AI capabilities include general AI (trained to perform including tasks outside their original domain or programming) and artificial superintelligence (exceeding the cognitive abilities of humans in all spheres of operation at speeds far exceeding human capability), introducing challenges for traditional operational planning methods.

EW systems based on artificial intelligence are susceptible to wrong data entry, with adverse effects (Davis 2019). Accidentally hitting the wrong targets can have strategic, social, and political implications.

One of the advantages of the EW system with AI is rapid decision-making, which can turn into a disadvantage if it unnecessarily hastens the end of the conflict before allowing the crisis to be managed through peace talks between the parties.

Machine learning cannot reliably predict the exact outcomes of an event, potentially inducing errors in decision-makers, jeopardizing their own strengths and proper handling of the situation.

AI-powered information warfare through fake news and photos and deep fakes can have adverse effects, distorting the public's and leaders' perception of the conflict.

Other possible vulnerabilities in the integration of artificial intelligence in electronic warfare:

- Vulnerabilities and exploitation:
    - Potential vulnerabilities in AI systems that adversaries can exploit.
    - The risk of AI-led attacks on critical infrastructure.
- Unwanted consequences:
    - Address potential unintended consequences of AI algorithms in dynamic electronic warfare scenarios.
    - Escalation risk due to autonomous AI decision-making.

Ethical considerations

The US is investing the most time and energy assessing how AI will impact the EW field by exploring issues such as ethics. According to col. P. J. Maykish, USAF, who served as director of analysis for the National Security Commission on Artificial Intelligence, "Ethics is a major consideration for U.S. AI development. It comes down to three issues: civil liberties, human rights and privacy." (Friedrich 2020) China and Russia do not share these concerns, Maykish recommending a " coalition of nations focused on common values." He also warns that if the US does not take into account the growth of AI and machine learning (ML) in other nations, it could fall behind in development compared to the achievements of others (Friedrich 2020).

Ethical considerations in approaching electronic warfare through the lens of artificial intelligence:

- Autonomous decision making:
  - o The ethical implications of allowing AI to make decisions in electronic warfare.
  - o Balancing human oversight with AI autonomy to prevent unintended consequences.
- Responsibility and accountability:
  - o Establishing clear lines of responsibility for actions based on artificial intelligence.
  - o Legal and ethical frameworks for addressing AI incidents in electronic warfare.

COGNITIVE EW

To access forbidden environments, EW systems must fully identify the signals of the adversary emitter and then quickly identify the appropriate technique to counter the threat. Cognitive systems take uncertainty into account and make recommendations or make decisions autonomously. The use of AI/ML is a critical component of cognitive EW. Cognitive EW can help identify jamming incidents, recognize, and classify the signal faster, and define the angle of arrival more quickly to determine the direction of the threat, recommending EW countermeasures (Gannon 2023).

Haigh and Andrusenko (Haigh and Andrusenko 2021) state that cognitive EW, by applying artificial intelligence (AI) to EW systems to enable adaptation and learning during a mission, is one of the critical advances that will determine the outcomes of future battles.

Cognitive radio concepts have been around since at least 1999, when Joe Mitola III (EASA 2020) introduced the term, and the idea of cognitive radar has been around since at least 2006 (DOD 2020).

A cognitive system, or intelligent agent, perceives its environment and takes actions to achieve its goals. Among the EW challenges from an AI perspective, Haigh and Andrusenko highlight (Haigh and Andrusenko 2021):

- Situation assessment for electronic support and assessment of battle damage in electronic warfare.

- Decision making for electronic attack, electronic protection, and electronic battle management.
- User requirements (access policies, performance, limitations).
- Connection between cognitive radio and EW systems.
- EW system design issues.

A fully cognitive EW system needs algorithmic advances for learning and inference, developments in decision making (DM), data management approaches, and architectures that support cognitive reasoning. The challenge of EW decision making is to build a cognitive controller that automatically maintains near-optimal configurations in highly dynamic environments.

Haigh and Andrusenko suggest a method for creating a basic EW cognitive system that can then be developed:

1. Choose a small task.
2. Choose an ML toolkit and prototype a model.
3. Evaluate with representative data.
4. Deploy on representative hardware. (Haigh and Andrusenko 2021)

Digital reprogramming of frequency and waveform modulation in radar technology is an evolving trend. This will make adversarial emitters harder to classify and identify (Adams 2018). EW cognitive systems are real-time learning and thinking systems. Their implementation requires low-power microprocessors and software tools capable of directing AI/ML systems in signal processing and recognition and guiding the systems' thought processes according to algorithms built for signal analysis and processing (J. Browne 2017). With the expansion of EW and radio. -frequency spectrum tools and systems, cognitive EW systems will be the tactical edge in maintaining the superiority of the electromagnetic spectrum (Gannon 2023).

CONCLUSION

Armed forces must use EW in new and innovative ways to overcome emerging threats. To communicate effectively and work together, the EMS must be harnessed at the national level, its control being decisive in any future conflict. EW can disrupt, deny, degrade, and deceive adversary systems. Gaining and maintaining an advantage in modern warfare requires a range of non-kinetic EW solutions that are more affordable and easier to maintain than kinetic solutions. In addition, emerging threats require new EW solutions that can significantly alter operations. EMS control and data are key to winning a conflict, and EW measures will ensure that control.

EW systems based on artificial intelligence play a very important role in rapidly adapting to the electromagnetic environment in warfare, increasing situational awareness and reliability of decisions. An AI-assisted EW system can be effective in identifying hostile radar emitters to determine the lethality of the threat so that an appropriate countermeasure strategy can be formulated to nullify the hostile threat. The information gathered can be used to develop a threat library for a possible electronic order of battle (EOB). Thus, artificial intelligence can provide planners with reliable tools for developing war plans.

The landscape of integrating AI into EW is changing rapidly and in potentially disruptive ways. Many experts want to ban autonomous weapons, but the complexity of the field requires that the ban be carefully enforced. An even more pressing issue in the near term is to fully understand the global implications of the shift in the power base of AI expertise from the military to commercial enterprises, so that experts become a critical commodity. Universities have been slow to respond to this demand, and governments and industry have lagged in providing financial incentives. Thus, the advance development of commercial information technology over the military sector, by attracting top talent and expanding autonomous systems capabilities, could be a double-edged sword that will undoubtedly affect defense around the world.

Whether it's about communications, radar, or some other system, any implementation of ML and AI is a challenge. The ideal testing process generates known results, so it's easy to check performance, but if a system learns and changes over time, there's no way to know in advance exactly what it will do.

Ultimately, the goal is to have autonomous systems that learn and make their own decisions to control operations in the EM spectrum.

Military forces are increasingly relying on technology in EW integrated with artificial intelligence. Finding the right balance between technological innovation, human oversight and security measures will determine the extent to which these benefits can be realized without compromising strategic objectives or ethical considerations. The transformative power of AI in EW has the potential to change the game. There is no shortage of questions to explore, but one thing is certain: the EW community must continue to embrace innovative thinking as we understand that the future battle will begin and end in the electromagnetic spectrum, and AI will play a critical role in this new era of modern warfare.

BIBLIOGRAPHY

* * *. 1984. *Voennyi Entsiklopedicheskii Slovar*. Moscova: Voennoe Izadatelstvo.

———. 1990. *Voenno-Morskoi Slovar*. Moscova: Voennoe Izadatelstvo.

———. 2000. "Electronic Warfare Fundamentals." https://falcon.blu3wolf.com/Docs/Electronic-Warfare-Fundamentals.pdf.

Adams, Charlotte. 2018. "Cognitive Electronic Warfare: Radio Frequency Spectrum Meets Machine Learning." 2018. //interactive.aviationtoday.com/avionicsmagazine/august-september-2018/cognitive-electronic-warfare-radio-frequency-spectrum-meets-machine-learning/.

Adamy, David. 2001. *EW 101: A First Course in Electronic Warfare*. Artech House.

AIM. 2019. "The AIM Initiative: A Strategy for Augmenting Intelligence Using Machines." 2019. https://www.dni.gov/index.php/newsroom/reports-publications/reports-publications-2019/3286-the-aim-initiative-a-strategy-for-augmenting-intelligence-using-machines.

Akhtar, Jabran, and Karl Erik Olsen. 2018. "A Neural Network Target Detector with Partial CA-CFAR Supervised Training." In *2018 International Conference on Radar (RADAR)*, 1–6. https://doi.org/10.1109/RADAR.2018.8557276.

Allen, Gregory C. 2019. *Understanding China's AI Strategy: Clues to Chinese Strategic Thinking on Artificial Intelligence and National Security*. Center for a New American Security.

Allen, John, and Giampiero Massolo. 2020. *The Global Race for Technological Superiority. Discover the Security Implication*. Edited by Fabio Rugge. Milan: Ledizioni.

Amuru, SaiDhiraj, Cem Tekin, Mihaela van der Schaar, and R. Michael Buehrer. 2015. "A Systematic Learning Method for Optimal Jamming." In *2015 IEEE International Conference on Communications (ICC)*, 2822–27. https://doi.org/10.1109/ICC.2015.7248754.

Army, United States Government US. 1996. "Joint Pub 3-58 Joint Doctrine for Military Deception." https://webharvest.gov/peth04/20041021042923/http://www.dti c.mil/doctrine/jel/new_pubs/jp3_58.pdf.

———. 2000. "Joint Publication 3-51 Joint Doctrine for Electronic Warfare." https://irp.fas.org/doddir/dod/jp3_51.pdf.

———. 2016. "Joint Publication JP 1-02 Department of Defense Dictionary of Military and Associated Terms." https://irp.fas.org/doddir/dod/jp1_02.pdf.

———. 2020a. *Joint Publication JP 3-13 Information Operations Change 1 November 2014*. Independently Published.

———. 2020b. "Joint Vision 2020: America's Military - Preparing for Tomorrow." https://apps.dtic.mil/sti/citations/ADA526044.

Baker, James E. 2018. "Artificial Intelligence and National Security Law: A Dangerous Nonchalance | MIT Center for International Studies." 2018. https://cis.mit.edu/publications/starr-forum-report/18-01-report.

Barshan, Billur, and Bahaeddin Eravci. 2012. "Automatic Radar Antenna Scan Type Recognition in Electronic Warfare." *IEEE Transactions on Aerospace and Electronic Systems* 48 (4): 2908–31. https://doi.org/10.1109/TAES.2012.6324669.

Bronk, Justin, Nick Reynolds, and Jack Watling. 2022. "The Russian Air War and Ukrainian Requirements for Air Defence." https://static.rusi.org/SR-Russian-Air-War-Ukraine-web-final.pdf.

Brooks, Risa. 2018. "Technology and Future War Will Test U.S. Civil-Military Relations." War on the Rocks. November 26, 2018. https://warontherocks.com/2018/11/technology-and-future-war-will-test-u-s-civil-military-relations/.

Browne, J. P. R., and Michael T. Thurbon. 1998. *Electronic Warfare*. Brassey's.

Browne, Jack. 2017. "Cognitive EW Provides Computer-Powered Protection." Microwaves & RF. May 10, 2017. https://www.mwrf.com/markets/defense/article/21848321/cogni tive-ew-provides-computerpowered-protection.

Brunt, Leroy B. Van. 1978. *Applied ECM*. EW Engineering.

BSI. 2023. "Federal Office for Information Security." Federal Office for Information Security. November 6, 2023. https://www.bsi.bund.de/EN/Home/home_node.html.

Butt, Faran, and Madiha Jalil. 2013. *An Overview of Electronic Warfare in Radar Systems*. https://doi.org/10.1109/TAEECE.2013.6557273.

Cameron, Lori. 2018. "Internet of Things Meets the Military and Battlefield: Connecting Gear and Biometric Wearables for an IoMT and IoBT." IEEE Computer Society. March 1, 2018. https://www.computer.org/publications/tech-news/research/internet-of-military-battlefield-things-iomt-iobt/.

Campen, Alan D. 1992. *The First Information War: The Story of Communications, Computers, and Intelligence Systems in the Persian Gulf War*. AFCEA International Press.

Carlin, John P. 2016. "Detect, Disrupt, Deter: A Whole-of-Government Approach to National Security Cyber Threats | CSIS Events." 2016. https://www.csis.org/events/detect-disrupt-deter-whole-government-approach-national-security-cyber-threats.

Casterline, Kyle A., Nicholas J. Watkins, Jon R. Ward, William Li, and Matthew J. Thommana. 2022. "Applications of Machine Learning for Electronic Warfare Emitter Identification and Resource Management." https://secwww.jhuapl.edu/techdigest/content/techdigest/pdf/V36-N02/36-02-Casterline.pdf.

Chen, Jian, Shiyou Xu, Jiangwei Zou, and Zengping Chen. 2019. "Interrupted-Sampling Repeater Jamming Suppression Based on Stacked Bidirectional Gated Recurrent Unit Network and Infinite Training." *IEEE Access* 7:107428–37. https://doi.org/10.1109/ACCESS.2019.2932793.

Clark, Colin. 2018. "Russia Widens EW War, 'Disabling' EC-130s OR AC-130s In Syria." *Breaking Defense* (blog). April 24, 2018. https://breakingdefense.sites.breakingmedia.com/2018/04/russia-widens-ew-war-disabling-ec-130s-in-syria/.

Coats, Daniel. 2021. "Intelligence Community Information Environment (IC IE) - Data Strategy." https://www.dni.gov/files/documents/CIO/Data-Strategy_2017-2021_Final.pdf.

Congressional Research Service. 2020. "Artificial Intelligence and National Security (R45178)." 2020. https://crsreports.congress.gov/product/details?prodcode=R45178.

Copp, Tara. 2021. "'It Failed Miserably': After Wargaming Loss, Joint Chiefs Are Overhauling How the US Military Will Fight." Defense One. July 26, 2021. https://www.defenseone.com/policy/2021/07/it-failed-miserably-after-wargaming-loss-joint-chiefs-are-overhauling-how-us-military-will-fight/184050/.

CRA. 2017. "Internet of Battlefield Things (IoBT) CRA – DEVCOM Army Research Laboratory." 2017. https://arl.devcom.army.mil/cras/iobt-cra/.

CRS. 2022. "Defense Primer: Electronic Warfare." https://sgp.fas.org/crs/natsec/IF11118.pdf.

CS Europe. 2023. "Cyber Security Europe | Cyber Security Insight for Boardroom and C-Suite Executives." Cyber Security Europe. 2023. https://www.cseurope.info/.

Davenport, Thomas, and Ravi Kalakota. 2019. "The Potential for Artificial Intelligence in Healthcare." *Future Healthc J* 6 (2): 94–98. https://doi.org/10.7861/futurehosp.6-2-94.

Davis, Zachary. 2019. "Artificial Intelligence on the Battlefield: Implications for Deterrence and Surprise." *PRISM* 8 (2): 114–31.

Day, Peter. 2016. "Peter Day's World of Business Podcast." 2016. http://downloads.bbc.co.uk/podcasts/radio/worldbiz/worldbiz_2 0150319-0730a.mp3.

De Spiegeleire, Stephan, Matthijs Maas, and Tim Sweijs. 2017. *Artificial Intelligence and the Future of Defense.*

Department of Defense. 2018. "Summary of the 2018 National Defense Strategy." https://dod.defense.gov/Portals/1/Documents/pubs/2018-National-Defense-Strategy-Summary.pdf.

Dickson, John R. V. 1987. "Electronic Warfare in Vietnam: Did We Learn Our Lessons?." In . https://www.semanticscholar.org/paper/Electronic-Warfare-in-Vietnam%3A-Did-We-Learn-Our-Dickson/399e7323fb081cb95db35d3a9d3075154a0de068.

DOD. 2020. "DoD Data Strategy." https://media.defense.gov/2020/Oct/08/2002514180/-1/-1/0/DOD-DATA-STRATEGY.PDF.

DoD. 2022. "DoD Announces Release of JADC2 Implementation Plan." U.S. Department of Defense. 2022. https://www.defense.gov/News/Releases/Release/Article/29700 94/dod-announces-release-of-jadc2-implementation-plan/https%3A%2F%2Fwww.defense.gov%2FNews%2FReleases %2FRelease%2FArticle%2F2970094%2Fdod-announces-release-of-jadc2-implementation-plan%2F.

Doskalov, Mikhail. 2013. "Perspektivy Razvitiia Sistemy Radioelektronnoi Borby Rossiiskoj Federatsii Na Period Do 2020 Goda." In *Oboronnyi Kompleks RF: Sostoianie i Razvitie.* http://federalbook.ru/files/OPK/Soderjanie/OPK-9/III/Doskalov.pdf.

Dudczyk, Janusz, and A. Kawalec. 2013. "Specific Emitter Identification Based on Graphical Representation of the Distribution of Radar Signal Parameters." *Jokull* 63 (November):408–16.

Duke, Audrey. 2023. "Harnessing Chaos: Unleashing Electromagnetic Warfare for Enhanced Joint Operations." https://apps.dtic.mil/sti/citations/AD1206172.

Dunn Cavelty, Myriam. 2012. "Cyber-Allies: Strengths and Weaknesses of NATO's Cyberdefense Posture." SSRN Scholarly Paper. Rochester, NY. https://papers.ssrn.com/abstract=1997153.

EASA. 2020. "Concepts of Design Assurance for Neural Networks (CoDANN)." https://www.easa.europa.eu/sites/default/files/dfu/EASA-DDLN-Concepts-of-Design-Assurance-for-Neural-Networks-CoDANN.pdf.

Elbir, Ahmet M., Kumar Vijay Mishra, and Yonina C. Eldar. 2019. "Cognitive Radar Antenna Selection via Deep Learning." arXiv. https://doi.org/10.48550/arXiv.1802.09736.

EMK, SU. 2023. "ECHO Network." 2023. https://echonetwork.eu/.

European Defence Agency. 2023. "Enhancing EU Military Capabilities Beyond 2040." https://eda.europa.eu/docs/default-source/eda-publications/enhancing-eu-military-capabilities-beyond-2040.pdf.

Freedberg, Sydney J. 2014. "US Has Lost 'Dominance In Electromagnetic Spectrum': Shaffer." *Breaking Defense* (blog). September 3, 2014. https://breakingdefense.com/2014/09/us-has-lost-dominance-in-electromagnetic-spectrum-shaffer/.

———. 2017. "Electronic Warfare 'Growing'; Joint Airborne EW Study Underway." *Breaking Defense* (blog). June 23, 2017. https://breakingdefense.sites.breakingmedia.com/2017/06/electronic-warfare-growing-joint-airborne-ew-study-underway/.

Friedrich, Nancy. 2020. "AI and Machine Learning Redefine the EW Landscape | 2020-12-08 | Microwave Journal." 2020. https://www.microwavejournal.com/articles/35107-ai-and-machine-learning-redefine-the-ew-landscape.

Fulghum, David A., and Robert Wall. 2007. "Israel Shows Electronic Prowess | Aviation Week Network." 2007. https://aviationweek.com/israel-shows-electronic-prowess.

Gambrell, Dorothy, and Charissa Isidro. 2022. "A Visual Guide to the World's Military Budgets." *Bloomberg.Com*, March 11, 2022. https://www.bloomberg.com/news/features/2022-03-11/the-largest-militaries-visualized.

Gannon, Brian P. 2023. "Implement AI in Electromagnetic Spectrum Operations." U.S. Naval Institute. August 1, 2023.

https://www.usni.org/magazines/proceedings/2023/august/imple
ment-ai-electromagnetic-spectrum-operations.

Gao, Jingpeng, Yi Lu, Junwei Qi, and Liangxi Shen. 2019. "A Radar Signal
Recognition System Based on Non-Negative Matrix Factorization
Network and Improved Artificial Bee Colony Algorithm." *IEEE
Access* 7:117612–26.
https://doi.org/10.1109/ACCESS.2019.2936669.

Gecgel Cetin, Selen, Caner Goztepe, and Gunes Karabulut Kurt. 2019.
*Jammer Detection Based on Artificial Neural Networks: A Measurement
Study.* https://doi.org/10.1145/3324921.3328788.

Gigova, Radina. 2017. "Who Putin Thinks Will Rule the World | CNN."
2017. https://edition.cnn.com/2017/09/01/world/putin-artificial-
intelligence-will-rule-world/index.html.

Goodfellow, Ian, Yoshua Bengio, and Aaron Courville. 2016. *Deep Learning:
Adaptive Computation and Machine Learning Series.* MIT Press.

Grant, P. M., and J. H. Collins. 1982. "Introduction to Electronic Warfare."
IEE Proceedings F (Communications, Radar and Signal Processing) 129 (3):
113–32. https://doi.org/10.1049/ip-f-1.1982.0020.

Gulhane, Tejaswi Singh and Amit. 2018. "8 Key Military Applications for
Artificial Intelligence." 2018. https://blog.marketresearch.com/8-
key-military-applications-for-artificial-intelligence-in-2018.

Guzenko, V. F., and A. L. Moraresku. 2017. *Radioelektronnaia Borba.
Sovremennoe Soderzhanie.* Moscova: Informatsionnyi Most.

Haigh, Karen Zita, and Julia Andrusenko. 2021. *Cognitive Electronic Warfare:
An Artificial Intelligence Approach.* Artech House.

Hamilton, Serena, A.J. Jakeman, and John Norton. 2008. "Artificial
Intelligence Techniques: An Introduction to Their Use for
Modelling Environmental Systems." *Mathematics and Computers in
Simulation* 78 (July):379–400.
https://doi.org/10.1016/j.matcom.2008.01.028.

Haney, Brian. 2019. "Applied Artificial Intelligence in Modern Warfare and
National Security Policy." SSRN Scholarly Paper. Rochester, NY.
https://doi.org/10.2139/ssrn.3454204.

Henney, Megan. 2019. "Big Tech Has Spent $582M Lobbying Congress.
Here's Where That Money Went." Text.Article. FOXBusiness. Fox
Business. May 8, 2019.
https://www.foxbusiness.com/technology/amazon-apple-
facebook-google-microsoft-lobbying-congress.

Hoehn, John. 2021. "Defense Primer: What Is Command and Control?"
https://apps.dtic.mil/sti/citations/AD1169627.

Insinna, Valerie. 2022. "China Could Obtain 1,500 Nuclear Warheads by
2035, Pentagon Estimates." *Breaking Defense* (blog). November 29,
2022.

https://breakingdefense.sites.breakingmedia.com/2022/11/china-to-obtain-1500-nuclear-warheads-by-2035-pentagon-estimates/.

Jankowicz, Mia. 2023. "Ukraine Is Losing 10,000 Drones a Month to Russian Electronic-Warfare Systems That Send Fake Signals and Screw with Their Navigation, Researchers Say." Business Insider. 2023. https://www.businessinsider.com/ukraine-losing-10000-drones-month-russia-electronic-warfare-rusi-report-2023-5.

Judd, Denis, and Keith Surridge. 2013. *The Boer War: A History*. Bloomsbury Academic.

Junfei, Yu, Li Jingwen, Sun Bing, and Jiang Yuming. 2018. "Barrage Jamming Detection and Classification Based on Convolutional Neural Network for Synthetic Aperture Radar." In *IGARSS 2018 - 2018 IEEE International Geoscience and Remote Sensing Symposium*, 4583–86. https://doi.org/10.1109/IGARSS.2018.8519373.

Kadlecová, Lucie, Nadia Meyer, Rafaël Cos, and Pauline Ravinet. 2020. "Mapping the Role of Science Diplomacy in the Cyber Field."

Kang, Li, Jiu Bo, Liu Hongwei, and Liang Siyuan. 2018. "Reinforcement Learning Based Anti-Jamming Frequency Hopping Strategies Design for Cognitive Radar." In *2018 IEEE International Conference on Signal Processing, Communications and Computing (ICSPCC)*, 1–5. https://doi.org/10.1109/ICSPCC.2018.8567751.

Katz, Yaakov. 2010. "And They Struck Them with Blindness." The Jerusalem Post | JPost.Com. September 29, 2010. https://www.jpost.com/magazine/features/and-they-struck-them-with-blindness.

Kjellén, Jonas. 2018. "Russian Electronic Warfare - The Role of Electronic Warfare in the Russian Armed Forces." https://web.archive.org/web/20181010174505/https://www.foi.s e/report-search/pdf?fileName=D%3A%5CReportSearch%5CFiles%5C4c5 47bec-bdfa-4bdb-a1c9-018097aaf615.pdf.

Kolesov, N. A., and I. G. Nasenkov. 2015. *Radioelektronnaia Borba. Ot Eksperimentov Proshlogo Do Reshayushchego Fronta Budushchego*. Moscova: Centre for Analysis of Strategies and Technologies (CAST).

Kolhatkar, Sheelah. 2019. "How Elizabeth Warren Came Up with a Plan to Break Up Big Tech." *The New Yorker*, August 20, 2019. https://www.newyorker.com/business/currency/how-elizabeth-warren-came-up-with-a-plan-to-break-up-big-tech.

Kott, Alexander. 2018. "Challenges and Characteristics of Intelligent Autonomy for Internet of Battle Things in Highly Adversarial Environments," March.

Kott, Alexander, David S. Alberts, and Cliff Wang. 2015. "Will Cybersecurity Dictate the Outcome of Future Wars?" *Computer* 48 (12): 98–101. https://doi.org/10.1109/MC.2015.359.

Krylov, G. O., S. L. Larionova, and Nikitina. 2017. *Bazovye Poniatiia Informatsionnoi Bezopasnosti.* Moscova: OOO RUSAJNS.

Kube, Courtney. 2018. "Russia Is Jamming American Drones in Syria, Officials Say." NBC News. April 10, 2018. https://www.nbcnews.com/news/military/russia-has-figured-out-how-jam-u-s-drones-syria-n863931.

Kucukozyigit, Ali. 2006. "Electronic Warfare (EW) Historical Perspectives and Its Relationship to Information Operations (IO) - Considerations for Turkey."

Lakhin, Andrei, and Andrei Korobeinikov. 2016. *Sostoianie i Perspektivy Razvitiia Voisk Radioelektronnoi Borby Vooruzhennykh Sil Rossiiskoi Federatsii.* Moscova: Informatsionnyi Most.

Lazarov, Lazar. 2019. "Perspectives and Trends for the Development of Electronic Warfare Systems." *2019 International Conference on Creative Business for Smart and Sustainable Growth (CREBUS)*, March, 1–3. https://doi.org/10.1109/CREBUS.2019.8840074.

Lee, Gyeong-Hoon, Jeil Jo, and Cheong Hee Park. 2020. "Jamming Prediction for Radar Signals Using Machine Learning Methods." *Security and Communication Networks* 2020 (January):e2151570. https://doi.org/10.1155/2020/2151570.

Li, Huiqin, Yanling Li, Chuan He, Jianwei Zhan, and Hui Zhang. 2021. "Cognitive Electronic Jamming Decision-Making Method Based on Improved Q -Learning Algorithm." *International Journal of Aerospace Engineering* 2021 (December):1–12. https://doi.org/10.1155/2021/8647386.

Li, Xueqiong, Zhitao Huang, Fenghua Wang, Xiang Wanga, and Tianrui Liu. 2018. "Toward Convolutional Neural Networks on Pulse Repetition Interval Modulation Recognition." *IEEE Communications Letters* PP (August):1–1. https://doi.org/10.1109/LCOMM.2018.2864725.

Li, Yangyang, Ximing Wang, Dianxiong Liu, Qiuju Guo, Xin Liu, Jie Zhang, and Yitao Xu. 2019. "On the Performance of Deep Reinforcement Learning-Based Anti-Jamming Method Confronting Intelligent Jammer." *Applied Sciences* 9 (7): 1361. https://doi.org/10.3390/app9071361.

Liao, Xiaofeng, Bo Li, and Bo Yang. 2018. "A Novel Classification and Identification Scheme of Emitter Signals Based on Ward's Clustering and Probabilistic Neural Networks with Correlation Analysis." *Computational Intelligence and Neuroscience* 2018 (November):e1458962. https://doi.org/10.1155/2018/1458962.

Liu, Yemin, Shiqi Xing, Y. Li, Dong Hou, and Wang Xuesong. 2017. "Jamming Recognition Method Based on the Polarization Scattering Characteristics of Chaff Clouds." *IET Radar, Sonar & Navigation* 11 (August). https://doi.org/10.1049/iet-rsn.2017.0121.

Liubin, Mikhail Dmitriyevich. 2009. "K Voprosu Ob Istorii Razvitiia i Perspektivakh Radioelektronnoi Borby." *Voennaia Mysl*, no. 3, 64–75.

Magrassi, Paolo. 2002a. *A World of Smart Objects: The Role of Auto-Identification Technologies.*

———. 2002b. *Why a Universal RFID Infrastructure Would Be a Good Thing.*

MarketsAndMarkets. 2023. "Artificial Intelligence (AI) in Military Market Size Growth Opportunities Industry Trends and Analysis 2030." MarketsandMarkets. 2023. https://www.marketsandmarkets.com/Market-Reports/artificial-intelligence-military-market-41793495.html.

Martino, Andrea De. 2012. *Introduction to Modern EW Systems.* Artech House.

McArthur, Charles W. 1990. *Operations Analysis in the United States Army Eighth Air Force in World War II.* American Mathematical Soc.

McDermott, Roger N. 2017. "Russia's Electronic Warfare Capabilities to 2025: Challenging NATO in the Electromagnetic Spectrum." ICDS. September 17, 2017. https://icds.ee/en/russias-electronic-warfare-capabilities-to-2025-challenging-nato-in-the-electromagnetic-spectrum/.

MeriTalk. 2018. "DARPA Floats a Proposal for the Ocean of Things." 2018. https://www.meritalk.com/articles/darpa-floats-a-proposal-for-the-ocean-of-things/.

Microwaves, Microwaves & RF. 2019. "BAE Bets on Use of Artificial Intelligence in Electronic Warfare." Microwaves & RF. July 15, 2019. https://www.mwrf.com/markets/defense/article/21849838/bae-systems-bae-bets-on-use-of-artificial-intelligence-in-electronic-warfare.

Ministry of Defence. 2021a. "Data Strategy for Defence." GOV.UK. 2021. https://www.gov.uk/government/publications/data-strategy-for-defence.

———. 2021b. "Digital Strategy for Defence." GOV.UK. 2021. https://www.gov.uk/government/publications/digital-strategy-for-defence-delivering-the-digital-backbone-and-unleashing-the-power-of-defences-data.

———. 2022. "Defence Artificial Intelligence Strategy." GOV.UK. 2022. https://www.gov.uk/government/publications/defence-artificial-intelligence-strategy/defence-artificial-intelligence-strategy.

Mizokami, Kyle. 2023. "Why Ukraine's GPS-Guided Bombs Keep Missing Their Targets." Popular Mechanics. April 20, 2023. https://www.popularmechanics.com/military/weapons/a4359169 4/russian-jamming-gps-guided-bombs/.

NATO. 2019. "The 107th NATO Electronic Warfare Advisory Committee (NEWAC) Convenes in Brussels." NATO. 2019. https://www.nato.int/cps/en/natohq/news_171280.htm.

———. 2023. "Electromagnetic Warfare." NATO. 2023. https://www.nato.int/cps/en/natohq/topics_80906.htm.

Neri, F. 1991. "Introduction to Electronic Defense Systems." In . https://www.semanticscholar.org/paper/Introduction-to-electronic-defense-systems-Neri/8d8aed6d92ecf7af850f09a2ee740380c2d4b366.

Noh, Sanguk, and Unseob Jeong. 2010. "Intelligent Command and Control Agent in Electronic Warfare Settings." *International Journal of Intelligent Systems* 25 (6): 514–28. https://doi.org/10.1002/int.20413.

Northrop. 2022. "Electronic Warfare and Sensors." https://info.breakingdefense.com/hubfs/E-Book_EW_&_Sensors_Northrop_Grumman_Breaking_Defense.pdf.

ODIN. 2023. "Borisoglebsk-2 (RB-301B) Russian Amphibious Multipurpose Jamming Complex." 2023. https://odin.tradoc.army.mil/WEG/Asset/Borisoglebsk-2_(RB-301B)_Russian_Amphibious_Multipurpose_Jamming_Complex.

Parker, Paul. 2018. "The Internet of Battlefield Things Is Coming. Are IT Pros Ready?" C4ISRNet. October 3, 2018. https://www.c4isrnet.com/opinion/2018/10/03/the-internet-of-battlefield-things-is-coming-are-it-pros-ready/.

Petrov, Nedyalko, Ivan Jordanov, and Jon Roe. 2013. "Radar Emitter Signals Recognition and Classification with Feedforward Networks." *Procedia Computer Science*, 17th International Conference in Knowledge Based and Intelligent Information and Engineering Systems - KES2013, 22 (January):1192–1200. https://doi.org/10.1016/j.procs.2013.09.206.

Poisel, Richard. 2008. *Introduction to Communication Electronic Warfare Systems.* Artech House.

Polit, Kate. 2018. "Army Takes on Wicked Problems With the Internet of Battlefield Things." 2018. https://www.meritalk.com/articles/army-takes-on-wicked-problems-with-the-internet-of-battlefield-things/.

Polmar, Norman. 1979. "The U. S. Navy: Electronic Warfare (Part 2)." U.S. Naval Institute. November 1, 1979.

https://www.usni.org/magazines/proceedings/1979/november/u
-s-navy-electronic-warfare-part-2.

Price, Alfred. 1984. *The History of US Electronic Warfare.* Association of Old
Crows.

Qiang, Xing, Zhu Wei-gang, and Bo Yuan. 2018. "Jamming Style Selection
for Small Sample Radar Jamming Rule Base." *2018 IEEE
International Conference on Signal Processing, Communications and
Computing (ICSPCC),* September, 1–5.
https://doi.org/10.1109/ICSPCC.2018.8567613.

Qu, Zhiyu, Wenyang Wang, Changbo Hou, and Chenfan Hou. 2019.
"Radar Signal Intra-Pulse Modulation Recognition Based on
Convolutional Denoising Autoencoder and Deep Convolutional
Neural Network." *IEEE Access* 7:112339–47.
https://doi.org/10.1109/ACCESS.2019.2935247.

Rahman, H. 2019. *Introduction to Electronic Defense Systems.* Boca Raton, FL,
USA: CRC Press.

Rambo. 2009. "Information Warfare: History of Electronic Warfare."
INFORMATION WARFARE (blog). December 7, 2009.
https://ew30.blogspot.com/2009/12/such-is-reliance-on-
electromagnetic-em.html.

Rogosa, Alexander. 2015. "Shifting Spaces: The Success of the SpaceX
Lawsuit and the Danger of Single-Source Contracts in America's
Space Program." *Federal Circuit Bar Journal* 25:101.

Rowlands, Greg. 2017. "The Internet of Military Things & Machine
Intelligence: A Winning Edge or Security Nightmare? | Australian
Army Research Centre (AARC)." 2017.
https://researchcentre.army.gov.au/library/land-power-
forum/internet-military-things-machine-intelligence-winning-edge-
or-security-nightmare.

Russell, Stephen, and Tarek Abdelzaher. 2018. "The Internet of Battlefield
Things: The Next Generation of Command, Control,
Communications and Intelligence (C3I) Decision-Making." In
*MILCOM 2018 - 2018 IEEE Military Communications Conference
(MILCOM),* 737–42.
https://doi.org/10.1109/MILCOM.2018.8599853.

Saxena, Shalini. 2017. "Researchers Create Electronic Rose Complete with
Wires and Supercapacitors." Ars Technica. March 1, 2017.
https://arstechnica.com/science/2017/03/researchers-grow-
electronic-rose-complete-with-wires-and-supercapacitors/.

Sfetcu, Nicolae. 2023a. "Evoluția inteligenței artificiale în domeniul
securității naționale." Intelligence Info. November 10, 2023.
https://www.intelligenceinfo.org/evolutia-inteligentei-artificiale-in-
domeniul-securitatii-nationale/.

————. 2023b. "Rolul serviciilor de informații în război." Intelligence Info. August 3, 2023. https://www.intelligenceinfo.org/rolul-serviciilor-de-informatii-in-razboi/.

————. 2024. "Războiul electronic și inteligența artificială." MultiMedia. January 8, 2024. https://www.telework.ro/ro/e-books/razboiul-electronic-si-inteligenta-artificiala/.

Shankar, M., and B. Mohan. 2013. "Recent Advances in Electronic Warfare-ESM Systems." In . https://www.semanticscholar.org/paper/RECENT-ADVANCES-IN-ELECTRONIC-WARFARE-ESM-SYSTEMS-Shankar-Mohan/bf6e4c372514695dd167eebf6f9dfb78ca120f6a.

Shao, Guangqing, Yushi Chen, and Yinsheng Wei. 2020. "Convolutional Neural Network-Based Radar Jamming Signal Classification With Sufficient and Limited Samples." *IEEE Access* 8:80588–98. https://doi.org/10.1109/ACCESS.2020.2990629.

Sharma, Purabi, Kandarpa Kumar Sarma, and Nikos E. Mastorakis. 2020. "Artificial Intelligence Aided Electronic Warfare Systems- Recent Trends and Evolving Applications." *IEEE Access* 8:224761–80. https://doi.org/10.1109/ACCESS.2020.3044453.

Silicon Labs. 2013. "The Evolution of Wireless Sensor Networks." https://www.silabs.com/documents/public/white-papers/evolution-of-wireless-sensor-networks.pdf.

Simonite, Tom. 2017. "Artificial Intelligence Fuels New Global Arms Race." *Wired*, 2017. https://www.wired.com/story/for-superpowers-artificial-intelligence-fuels-new-global-arms-race/.

Singer, Peter W., and Allan Friedman. 2014. *Cybersecurity: What Everyone Needs to Know.* OUP USA.

Singh, Mohinder. 1988. "Electronic Warfare." https://www.drdo.gov.in/sites/default/files/publcations-document/Electronic%20Warfare.pdf.

Skolnik, Merrill I. 2008. *Radar Handbook, Third Edition.* McGraw-Hill Education.

Smith, Craig. 2019. "Eye On AI." Eye On AI. August 28, 2019. https://www.eye-on.ai.

Smith, Patrick. 2022. *Russian Electronic Warfare: A Growing Threat to U.S. Battlefield Supremacy.* American Security Project.

Smith, Ron, and Scott Knight. 2005. "Applying Electronic Warfare Solutions to Network Security - Canadian Military Journal." 2005. http://www.journal.forces.gc.ca/vo6/no3/electron-eng.asp.

SPARTA. 2023. "SPARTA Consortium." 2023. https://www.cybersecurityintelligence.com/sparta-consortium-5594.html.

Stackpole, Beth. 2016. "Keeping the Connected Soldier Connected with Simulation." Digital Engineering. September 1, 2016. https://www.digitalengineering247.com/article/keeping-the-connected-soldier-connected-with-simulation.

State Council. 2017. "A Next Generation Artificial Intelligence Development Plan." *China Copyright and Media* (blog). July 20, 2017. https://chinacopyrightandmedia.wordpress.com/2017/07/20/a-next-generation-artificial-intelligence-development-plan/.

Sydney J. Freedberg Jr. 2020. "Project Rainmaker: Army Weaves 'Data Fabric' To Link Joint Networks." *Breaking Defense* (blog). November 17, 2020. https://breakingdefense.sites.breakingmedia.com/2020/11/project-rainmaker-army-weaves-data-fabric-to-link-joint-networks/.

Taddeo, Mariarosaria. 2012. "An Analysis for a Just Cyber Warfare." In *2012 4th International Conference on Cyber Conflict (CYCON 2012)*, 1–10. https://ieeexplore.ieee.org/document/6243976.

Tang, Author: Hazel. 2020. "Preparing for the Future of Artificial Intelligence. Executive Office of the President: National Science and Technology Council and Committee on Technology. October, 2016." *AIMed* (blog). April 9, 2020. https://ai-med.io/executive/preparing-for-the-future-of-artificial-intelligence-executive-office-of-the-president-national-science-and-technology-council-and-committee-on-technology-october-2016/.

Tegler, Eric. 2022. "The Vulnerability of AI Systems May Explain Why Russia Isn't Using Them Extensively in Ukraine." Forbes. 2022. https://www.forbes.com/sites/erictegler/2022/03/16/the-vulnerability-of-artificial-intelligence-systems-may-explain-why-they-havent-been-used-extensively-in-ukraine/.

Tegmark, Max. 2018. "Life 3.0: Being Human in the Age of Artificial Intelligence | Mitpressbookstore." July 31, 2018. https://mitpressbookstore.mit.edu/book/9781101970317.

Tsui, Chi-Hao Cheng, James. 2022. *An Introduction to Electronic Warfare; from the First Jamming to Machine Learning Techniques*. New York: River Publishers. https://doi.org/10.1201/9781003337171.

Tucker, Patrick. 2022. "AI Is Already Learning from Russia's War in Ukraine, DOD Says." Defense One. April 21, 2022. https://www.defenseone.com/technology/2022/04/ai-already-learning-russias-war-ukraine-dod-says/365978/.

US Marine Corps. 2016. "Electronic Warfare." https://www.marines.mil/Portals/1/Publications/MCRP%203-32D.1%20(Formerly%20MCWP%203-40.5).pdf.

Vincent, James. 2017. "Elon Musk and AI Leaders Call for a Ban on Killer Robots." The Verge. August 21, 2017.

https://www.theverge.com/2017/8/21/16177828/killer-robots-ban-elon-musk-un-petition.

Waghray, Namrita, and P. M. Menghal. 2011. "Simulation of Radar Topology Networks to Evolve the Electronic Warfare Survivability Metrics." *2011 3rd International Conference on Electronics Computer Technology,* April, 355–59. https://doi.org/10.1109/ICECTECH.2011.5941622.

Wan, Tao, Xinying Fu, Kaili Jiang, Yuan Zhao, and Bin Tang. 2019. "Radar Antenna Scan Pattern Intelligent Recognition Using Visibility Graph." *IEEE Access* 7:175628–41. https://doi.org/10.1109/ACCESS.2019.2957769.

Wang, Feng, Shanshan Huang, Hao Wang, and Chenlu Yang. 2018. "Automatic Modulation Classification Exploiting Hybrid Machine Learning Network." *Mathematical Problems in Engineering* 2018 (December):e6152010. https://doi.org/10.1155/2018/6152010.

Wei, Dongxu, Shuning Zhang, Si Chen, Huichang Zhao, and Linzhi Zhu. 2019. "Research on Deception Jamming of Chaotic Composite Short-Range Detection System Based on Bispectral Analysis and Genetic Algorithm–Back Propagation." *International Journal of Distributed Sensor Networks* 15 (5): 1550147719847444. https://doi.org/10.1177/1550147719847444.

Weisgerber, Marcus. 2017. "The Pentagon's New Algorithmic Warfare Cell Gets Its First Mission: Hunt ISIS." Defense One. May 14, 2017. https://www.defenseone.com/technology/2017/05/pentagons-new-algorithmic-warfare-cell-gets-its-first-mission-hunt-isis/137833/.

Yasar, Nurgul, Fatih Mustafa Yasar, and Yucel Topcu. 2012. "Operational Advantages of Using Cyber Electronic Warfare (CEW) in the Battlefield." In *Cyber Sensing 2012*, 8408:151–59. SPIE. https://doi.org/10.1117/12.919454.

You, Shixun, Ming Diao, and Lipeng Gao. 2019. "Deep Reinforcement Learning for Target Searching in Cognitive Electronic Warfare." *IEEE Access* 7:37432–47. https://doi.org/10.1109/ACCESS.2019.2905649.

Zhang, Ming, Ming Diao, Lipeng Gao, and Lutao Liu. 2017. "Neural Networks for Radar Waveform Recognition." *Symmetry* 9 (5): 75. https://doi.org/10.3390/sym9050075.

www.ingramcontent.com/pod-product-compliance
Lightning Source LLC
LaVergne TN
LVHW051749050326
832903LV00029B/2805